How to Make Money with Real Estate Options

HOW TO MAKE MONEY WITH REAL ESTATE OPTIONS

Low-Cost, Low-Risk, High-Profit Strategies for Controlling Undervalued Property . . . without the Burdens of Ownership!

THOMAS J. LUCIER

WILEY

John Wiley & Sons, Inc.

Published by John Wiley & Sons, Inc., Hoboken, New Jersey.
Published simultaneously in Canada.

For general information on our other products and services please contact our Customer Care Department within the United States at (800) 762-2974, outside the United States at (317) 572-3993 or fax (317) 572-4002.

Wiley also publishes its books in a variety of electronic formats. Some content that appears in print may not be available in electronic books. For more information about Wiley products, visit our web site at www.wiley.com.

Library of Congress Cataloging-in-Publication Data:

Lucier, Thomas J.
  How to make money with real estate options : low-cost, low-risk,
high-profit strategies for controlling undervalued property . . . without the
burdens of ownership! / Thomas J. Lucier.
    p. cm.
  ISBN 0-471-69276-X (paper)
  1. Real estate investment—United States. 2. Option (Contract)—United
States. 3. House buying—United States. I. Title.
  HD255.L827 2005
  332.63′24—dc22
                                                        2004021919

Printed in the United States of America.

10 9 8 7 6 5 4 3 2 1

To my grandson,
Zachary W. Johnson, Poppy's boy

CONTENTS

set up a home office for your option investment business.
• Why you shouldn't form a separate business entity before
you do any deals.

PART II
FIVE REALISTIC STRATEGIES THAT YOU CAN USE TO MAKE MONEY WITH REAL ESTATE OPTIONS TODAY

Why properties with curable obsolescent flaws make ideal option properties. • The three types of obsolescent flaws that cause properties to lose value. • How obsolescent properties can be put to their most profitable use. • Why option investors are usually buyers of last resort for obsolescent property. • What you should check for when you come across an obsolescent property. • Why you must be able to think outside your local real estate market.

Why most of the lease and option strategies being taught today are not profitable. • How a lease and option transaction works. • Why you must always use separate lease and real estate option agreements. • Six key terms that must be negotiated in all lease and option agreements. • The best type of house to use the lease and option strategy on. • The property owners who are most likely to agree to a lease and option deal. • Memorandum of Lease Agreement

Six main conditions that cause property problems. • Why government agencies can be an excellent source of problem property leads. • The two types of problem property owners you are most likely to encounter. • Three types of problem properties that scare off most conventional investors. • Why properties with problems that require specialized knowledge to solve are the most profitable.

How the rezoning process works in most jurisdictions. • What you must include in your rezoning application package. • Why you must know who the anti-rezoning zealots are in your area. • How to quickly determine if a potential option property can be rezoned. • Why it's best to take the path of least resistance when applying for rezoning approval. • What you need to do when buying an option on a property you want rezoned.

PART III
A 12-STEP PROCESS FOR BUYING AND RESELLING REAL ESTATE OPTIONS

▰ LIST OF DOWNLOADABLE FORMS ▰

Real Estate Options:
What They Are, How They Work, and
Why You Should Use Them

I first want to thank you for investing your money in a copy of *How to Make Money with Real Estate Options*. This one-of-a-kind book was written for serious, rational, reasonable, intelligent, reality-based, goal-driven, and action-oriented adults who are willing to take calculated risks in order to profit from the many money-making opportunities that real estate options provide today. I am a firm believer that a real how-to book should tell its readers precisely what to do while providing detailed instructions on exactly how to do it. I also believe that a how-to book should live up to its title. And I am very confident that this unique book will exceed your expectations on both counts! As you will soon find out, it is packed with step-by-step instructions, ready-to-use worksheets, checklists, letters and agreements, and practical, no-nonsense advice on how to use real estate options to control undervalued properties with immediate resale profit potential.

Learning about Real Estate Options

When I first got interested in using real estate options in 1985, there were no publications available like this book. The scant amount of information that I was about to scrounge up about real estate options told me just enough to be dangerous, but not enough so that I really knew what I was doing. This lack of solid information meant that I did not have the luxury of learning from someone else's mistakes. I had no choice but to go it alone. So, how did I become my own real estate option expert? I did it the old-fashioned way. I went out on my own and learned the hard way how real estate options really work. I did a lot of research, talked to a lot of knowledgeable people, and asked a lot of questions. Then, I went out and bought some real estate options and made the inevitable mistakes, which I learned from. And while all of this was going on, I took copious notes to keep track of my trials, tribulations, numerous mistakes, and firsthand experiences as a real estate option investor. Those notes are the basis for this book.

What You Need to Know about Real Estate Options

Real estate options are a little known and seldom used investment strategy probably because the only time that most people ever read or hear anything about real estate options is when they are bandied about, willy-nilly, on real estate web site message boards or discussed at real estate investment club meetings by people whose collective knowledge of the subject would not fill a thimble. However, when fully understood, properly prepared, and used correctly, real estate options are an excellent way to conserve capital, create leverage, reduce risks, and gain control of properties with immediate resale profit potential. But, to avoid the potential problems and pitfalls that plague most uninformed and unsuspecting real estate option investors, you first need to know:

1. The difference between a straight or naked real estate option and a lease-option.
2. What a real estate option is.
3. The seven elements of a real estate option transaction.
4. How a real estate option transaction works.
5. The legal status of real estate options in your state.

The Difference between a Straight Real Estate Option and a Lease-Option

First things first: There is a world of difference between the straight or naked real estate options that I am writing about in this book and the rather ubiquitous lease-options that everyone and their brother has written about over the past 10 years. For starters, the real estate option agreement that I am writing about is a stand-alone document, which is not part of a lease agreement. Second, under the terms of a lease-option agreement, the lessee-optionee takes possession of the property under lease and is legally obligated to pay a monthly lease payment. The only payment required on a real estate option is a one-time option consideration fee. And unlike real estate options, lease-options violate the loan due-on-sale clause contained in residential mortgage or deed of trust loans. In other words, in the event that a lender discovers that a property owner has entered into a lease-option agreement, the lender could call the mortgage or deed of trust loan due and foreclose if the loan was not paid off in full.

Often, people confuse a real estate option with a right of first refusal. The main difference between a straight or naked real estate option and a right of first refusal is that a right of first refusal is the right to match a bona fide purchase offer from a third party, whereas a real estate option is an irrevocable right to purchase property, usually at a pre-determined price, within a specified time period. For example, most commercial leases include a right of first refusal that gives the lessee the right to match any written offers that the owner may receive to purchase the property under lease.

The Definition of a Real Estate Option

In general legal terms, a real estate option grants the party owning the option, the optionee, the exclusive, unrestricted, and irrevocable right to purchase property from the party selling the option, the optionor, during the specified period of time that the real estate option is in effect.

A Real Estate Option Grants Only an Irrevocable Right to Purchase Property

I want to state right from the get-go that the only thing that a straight or naked real estate option grants is an irrevocable right to purchase the property under option within the option period. Nothing more! An optionee has absolutely no beneficial or equitable interest whatsoever in a property under option. Furthermore, in my professional opinion, the creation and sale of a straight or naked real estate option does not violate the due-on-sale clause contained in government-backed and conventional mortgage or deed of trust loans secured by a lien on residential property containing five or fewer units. Again, in my professional opinion, there is absolutely no way that any lender can legally exercise its option pursuant to a due-on-sale clause on discovering the creation and sale of a straight or naked real estate option. Why do I hold this opinion? Because Title 12 of the Code of Federal Regulations refers specifically to lease-option contracts, but makes no mention whatsoever of straight or naked real estate option to purchase contracts. Real estate options are not covered under Section 591.2 (b) of the Code of Federal Regulations that defines the due-on-sale clause as follows:

> Due-on-sale clause means a contract provision which authorizes the lender, at its option, to declare immediately due and payable sums secured by the lender's security instrument upon a sale or transfer of all or any part of the real property securing the loan without the lender's prior written consent. For purposes of this definition, a sale or transfer means the conveyance of real property or any right, title or interest therein, whether legal or equitable, whether voluntary or, by outright sale, deed, installment sale contract, land contract, contract for deed, leasehold interest with a term greater than three years, lease-option contract or any other method of conveyance of real property interests.

Furthermore, the creation and sale of a straight or naked real estate option does not transfer any legal or beneficial interest in the property under option until after the option is exercised. The transfer of the property or a beneficial interest in borrower is the standard loan due-on-sale covenant, which is included in all Fannie Mae and Freddie Mac conventional residential mortgage and deed of trust loan documents. It states in part:

> "Interest in the Property" means any legal or beneficial interest in the Property, including, but not limited to, those beneficial interests transferred in a bond for deed, contract for deed, installment sales contract or escrow agreement, the intent of which is the transfer of title by Borrower at a future date to a purchaser.

During the course of researching this book, I found no court cases nationwide in which a residential lender has exercised its loan's due-on-sale clause and declared a loan to be in default upon discovering that the borrower had created and sold a straight or naked real estate option on the property securing the mortgage or deed of trust and promissory note.

The due-on-sale clauses included in almost all commercial mortgage or deed of trust loans do not specifically prohibit the creation and sale of a straight or naked real estate option on the property securing the mortgage or deed of trust and promissory note. The fact is that other than government-backed multifamily loans, most commercial mortgage or deed of trust loans are one-of-a-kind loan instruments written specifically for the property securing the loan and almost never contain any prohibition against creating and selling a real estate option.

Real Estate Options and the Doctrine of Equitable Conversion

Under what is known as the *doctrine of equitable conversion,* once a real estate purchase agreement is signed by all parties and becomes effective, the buyer becomes the equitable owner and the seller retains bare legal title to the property under agreement. However, under a real estate option, the equitable conversion does not occur until after the option is exercised and not when the real estate option agreement is signed by all parties and becomes effective. This is because there is no legal obligation to buy and sell until after a real estate option is exercised. After a real estate option is exercised, the optionee-buyer retains equitable ownership of the property.

The difference between a real estate option agreement and a standard purchase agreement is that there is no contractual obligation to purchase the property. For example, when a buyer and seller sign a purchase agreement, they become legally obligated to buy and sell the property under contract, and either party can be sued if he or she fails to do so. However, when an optionee and optionor sign a real estate option agreement, the optionee has no contractual obligation to purchase the property under option. An optionee can let a real estate option expire, and an optionor has no legal recourse against the optionee.

Why a Straight Real Estate Option Agreement Is Not an Executory Contract

An executory contract is generally defined as: "a contract where both parties have an obligation to perform in the future." And state and federal courts nationwide have traditionally held the view that straight or naked real estate options are unilateral contracts, under which the obligation to perform rests solely on the optionor, while the optionee is under no obligation to do anything whatsoever. The only notable exception to this is when an option agreement is included in a federal bankruptcy petition and the optionee has notified the optionor of his or her intention to exercise the option prior to the bankruptcy petition being filed.

The Seven Key Elements of a Real Estate Option Transaction

A real estate option transaction consists of the following seven key elements:

1. *Optionee:* Optionee is the party buying a real estate option. Once a real estate option is exercised, the optionee becomes the buyer.

2. *Optionor:* Optionor is the party selling a real estate option. Once a real estate option is exercised, the optionor becomes the seller.

3. *Real estate option:* When an optionee buys a real estate option, he or she buys an exclusive, unrestricted, and irrevocable right and option to purchase a property at a fixed purchase price within a specified option period.

4. *Option consideration:* Option consideration is the amount of money paid by an optionee to buy a real estate option from an optionor.

5. *Option period:* The option period is the specific period of time stated in the real estate option agreement in which the option is in effect.

6. *Exercise of option:* The exercising of a real estate option occurs when the optionee notifies the optionor, in writing, that he or she is going to exercise the real estate option and purchase the property under option.

7. *Expiration of option:* A real estate option expires when an optionee fails to exercise his or her real estate option within the option period stated in the real estate option agreement.

How a Real Estate Option Transaction Works

Here is a sequential outline of the mechanics of a real estate option transaction:

Step 1: The optionee pays a real estate option fee to the optionor.

Step 2: The optionor grants the optionee the exclusive, unrestricted, and irrevocable right and option to purchase a property at a fixed purchase price during the option period by executing a real estate option agreement with the optionee.

Step 3: The optionee assigns or exercises his or her real estate option or lets it expire.

Step 4: Once exercised, a real estate option agreement turns into a bilateral agreement in which the optionee becomes the buyer and the optionor becomes the seller.

Step 5: The seller transfers the property's title to the buyer at the closing.

The Legal Status of Real Estate Options Varies from State to State

Unfortunately, there's no Uniform Commercial Code equivalent for real estate options. The legal status of real estate options varies from state to state. In most states, the legal status of real estate options has evolved over the years from a combination of common and case law. The case law that regulates estate options in most states is the result of various lawsuits involving legal disputes between optionees and optionors over the use of real estate options. To know the legal status of real estate options in your state, you should consult with a board-certified real estate attorney who is familiar with how real estate options work in your state. I suggest that you ask your real estate attorney the following four questions:

1. What constitutes a valid and fully enforceable real estate option agreement?
2. Does a real estate option, prior to its being exercised, create an estate in land?
3. Can a real estate option be recorded in the public records so it constitutes constructive notice?
4. Does a real estate option violate any rule against perpetuities that your state may have?

In some states, most notably California, courts have ruled that real estate options are personal property rather than real property. For example, in a federal bankruptcy case, *In re Merten*, 164 B.R. 641 (Bankr. S.D. Cal. 1994), the court ruled that under applicable California law, an unexercised option to purchase real estate is *personalty*—personal property—and not *realty*—real property. I suggest that you check with a real estate attorney to find out if real estate options are considered to be personalty or realty in your state. Your state's real property statutes should be available online via the Internet or at your county's public law library. If there is not a public law library in your area, check with your local public library to see if they have a current copy of your state's civil statutes. A listing of state statutes, by subject, is available at the following web site: www.law.cornell.edu/topics/state_statutes.html.

No Licensing Requirement to Buy and Sell Options for Your Own Account

Every once and awhile, I will read on the Internet that a private individual investor, acting as a principal on his or her own behalf, must have a real estate salesperson's license to buy and sell real estate options. This is unadulterated bullspit! The fact of the matter is that there are no states that have licensing requirements for private individual investors who act as a principal when buying and selling real estate options.

Why You Should Add Real Estate Options to Your Repertoire of Strategies

Typically, many real estate options are bought more on speculation than on anything else. However, buying real estate options on speculation is not what this book is about. If you follow the advice contained in this book, all you should be doing is changing your name from buyer to real estate optionee. When used properly on the right types of undervalued properties, real estate options provide an excellent low-cost, low-risk, high-profit potential property control technique, which knowledgeable, savvy investors should add to their repertoire of real estate investment strategies. The real estate option strategies outlined in this book are based on a very simple concept:

1. Buy a low-cost real estate option on an undervalued property with immediate resale profit potential.
2. Package the property under option to highlight its best future use.
3. Market the property under option on the Internet to potential buyers worldwide.
4. Sell the real estate option on the property for maximum profit.

Twenty-Four Good Reasons to Buy Options Instead of Properties

I am willing to bet anyone an ice cold case of Beck's Beer that the numerous commercial real estate market meltdowns that have occurred during the past 30 years would not have been so severe if the high rollers had bought more real estate options instead of properties. In this way, if they did not want to exercise their real estate options, they could have simply let them expire, and that would have been the end of it. And they would not have incurred any of the transaction, maintenance, management, holding, and debt service costs that eventually forced them to go belly-up. In other words, they would not have been saddled with the financial responsibility and personal liability that go along with outright property ownership, and they automatically would have avoided having to:

1. Fill out intrusive loan applications.
2. Qualify for new loans.
3. Make monthly loan payments.

4. Circumvent loan due-on-sale clauses.
5. Worry about liability lawsuits.
6. Support negative cash flows.
7. Contemplate being foreclosed on.
8. Collect tenant rental payments.
9. File tenant eviction lawsuits.
10. Chase deadbeat tenants.
11. Go into debt.
12. Buy any property.
13. Pay outrageous loan fees.
14. Assume existing loans.
15. Make expensive property repairs.
16. Babysit tenants.
17. Fret over escalating property taxes.
18. Fill vacancies.
19. Pay exorbitant property insurance premiums.
20. Maintain property and tenant records.
21. Clean up after messy tenants.
22. Pay transaction costs.
23. Assume financial and personal liability.
24. Manage property.

Potential Risks That You Cannot Control When Using Real Estate Options

Although I consider the use of real estate options to be a relatively low-risk investment strategy, there are potential risks that you cannot control when using real estate options. For example, the property under option could be:

1. Foreclosed on.
2. Placed under the control of a federal bankruptcy court trustee.
3. Condemned by a government agency under the right of eminent domain.
4. Destroyed by fire, storm, or earthquake.
5. Taken as part of a government asset forfeiture lawsuit.

When I was starting out as an option investor, I bought a one-year option on a run-down commercial property in Ruskin, Florida, that belonged to a fertilizer manufacturer. And two months later, the company filed for protection under Chapter 11 of the U.S. Bankruptcy Code, and the property I owned an option on came under the control of a court-appointed bankruptcy trustee. The judge presiding over the case in U.S. Bankruptcy Court in Tampa ruled that my real estate option to purchase agreement was personalty or personal property and that I did not have an interest in the property. The case dragged on for over two years and, in the meantime, my option expired and I was out my $3,500 option fee. The $3,500 lesson that I learned here was to always do a lawsuit search on the individual or business entity that owns the property before I ever plunk down my hard-earned money to buy an option.

Use This Book to Become Your Own Real Estate Option Expert

I want you to use this book to educate yourself so that you become your own real estate option expert. I say this because there are very few sources of reliable information and advice, other than this book, available on straight or naked real estate options. My experiences have shown me that many of the people who claim to know all about real estate options really do not know diddly squat about the subject. Case in point: When I first started using options, I had a title agent swear up and down to me that I was required to purchase documentary tax stamps whenever I recorded a memorandum of a real estate option agreement in the public records of my county, Hillsborough County, Florida. This sounded rather farfetched to me because in Florida, documentary tax stamps must be purchased only when there is an actual transfer of a property's title. So, I called the manager at the Hillsborough County Clerk of the Circuit Court Recording Department and asked her about it. Guess what? Just as I had suspected, the title agent was chock-full of what makes the grass grow greener. From that point on, I stopped using title companies and started using a board-certified real estate attorney who was very well versed on the inner workings of real estate options. I also learned a very valuable lesson: When it comes to advice on real estate options, trust no one, assume nothing, verify everything, and be prepared for anything. In this business, you just cannot afford to blindly rely on the advice given to you by so-called experts. You must be able to verify everything your advisers tell you. And if you cannot confirm that what you are being told to do is correct, there is an excellent chance that you will end up being what I call a mushroom investor—an investor who is kept in the dark and fed a lot of bullspit by his or her advisers!

Twelve Sound Rules That You Should Follow as a Real Estate Option Investor

Finally, this introduction would not be complete if I did not include the following 12 sound rules that you should follow as a real estate option investor:

Rule 1: Know what you do not know.

Rule 2: Do not buy problems that you cannot solve.

Rule 3: Make your profit when you buy.

Rule 4: Have an exit strategy before you enter into a deal.

Rule 5: Anticipate situations before they become problems.

Rule 6: Concentrate on doing what you do best.

Rule 7: Set a goal, make a plan, and work hard.

Rule 8: Always take the path of least resistance.

Rule 9: Buy locally and sell globally.

Rule 10: Avoid doing business through third parties.

Rule 11: Assume nothing, verify everything, and be prepared for anything.

Rule 12: Do what you say you are going to do when you say you are going to do it.

How to Contact the Author

Please feel free to contact me if there is something that you still do not understand after reading this book twice. Unlike 99 percent of all real estate authors in America today, there are no gatekeepers between my readers and me. I answer my own e-mail and telephone, and I am fully wired to communicate from anywhere within the United States. You can e-mail me directly at tjlucier@thomaslucier.com. Or, you can call me direct at my office in Tampa, Florida, at (813) 237-6267. No other real estate author offers his or her readers this free service!

PART I

HOW YOU CAN MAKE MONEY IN REAL ESTATE TODAY WITHOUT EVER BUYING ANY PROPERTY

Why Real Estate Options Are Less Risky, More Profitable, and Easier to Use Than Most Property-Flipping Strategies Being Taught Today

The problem with 99 percent of all the property-flipping strategies being taught today is that they require would-be real estate mavens to go out on buying binges and scarf up properties like they are going out of style and thus become financially responsible for monthly loan payments and property repairs. But for many people who want to profit from real estate, outright property ownership is too expensive, too time consuming, and far too risky. They crave a low-cost, low-risk way to make money in real estate, without ever having to buy any property. And this is exactly where little known and seldom used real estate options come into play. Options provide the ideal strategy for people who want to be part-time investors because they do not have a lot of money or time to spend on real estate. Plus, options are an excellent way for savvy investors to create leverage, reduce risk, and conserve capital, while holding the controlling interest in a piece of undervalued property. Real estate options also act to level the playing field by providing individual investors with a low-cost way to gain the controlling interest in large properties that they would not be able to buy outright. Over the years, high-profile investors such as Donald Trump, Walt Disney, and Trammell Crow have successfully used real estate options to assemble large tracts of land for future development. In this chapter, I give you the inside scoop on exactly why most of the property-flipping strategies being taught today are way too expensive and hard to implement and why it makes much more financial sense to flip a real estate option instead of a property.

The Definition of Property Flipping

Before I go any further, you first need to know what the term *property flipping* means. Property flipping is generally defined within the real estate investment industry as: "the process of buying a property and quickly reselling it for a profit."

Today, thanks in large part to news reports by the media, the term property flipping has pretty much become synonymous with fraud. But contrary to what many uninformed members of the media would want the American public to believe, there is absolutely nothing illegal, immoral, or unethical about making an honest profit from legitimately flipping a piece of property. It is called *capitalism* and is what our economic system is based on. And I happen to be an unabashed capitalist and damn proud of it!

The HUD Rule Prohibiting Predatory Property Flipping with FHA Loans

The U.S. Department of Housing and Urban Renewal (HUD) defines *predatory property flipping* as: "the practice whereby a property recently acquired is resold for a considerable profit with an artificially inflated value, often abetted by a lender's collusion with the appraiser." And on June 2, 2003, HUD imposed a rule that places time restrictions on the resale of properties financed by Federal Housing Authority (FHA) loans. This was done in an effort to try to curb predatory lenders and dishonest real estate investors from ripping off unsuspecting home-buyers by reselling or flipping properties at artificially inflated sale prices. However, as far as I am concerned, the only thing that this rule has accomplished is to stop honest investors from using FHA loans. I suspect that crooked investors, appraisers, and lenders are still using FHA loans to perpetrate fraud; they are just using more sophisticated scams, which HUD has not caught on to yet! For a detailed explanation of HUD's rule against predatory property flipping, log on to the following web site: www.florida.ctic.com/bulletins/2003/2003-03.pdf

Why Most Property-Flipping Transactions Are under Intense Scrutiny

Nowadays, because of the media and the hullabaloo surrounding the action taken by HUD, just about every property-flipping transaction is put under the microscope by lenders and title and escrow agents before they will agree to finance and close the deal. The reason for this intense scrutiny is that lenders and title and escrow agents are constantly on the lookout for fraudulent property-flipping schemes, which cost them millions of dollars annually. Most of the property-flipping shenanigans involve collusive relationships among investors, property appraisers, and mortgage brokers. In a typical property-flipping scam, a dishonest investor:

1. Buys a low-cost run-down property in a low-income neighborhood.
2. Buys an inflated property appraisal report from an unscrupulous property appraiser.
3. Steers an unsophisticated buyer to a crooked mortgage broker, who prepares a fraudulent loan application to obtain a mortgage or deed of trust loan from an unsuspecting lender to finance the purchase of a grossly over-priced property.

This type of fraudulent property-flipping transaction usually ends up in foreclosure because the new owner cannot afford to make the loan payments and pay for needed property repairs, too. And in most cases, the American taxpayer winds up getting stuck paying off the government-backed loan that was used to finance the scam.

Five Obstacles That Investors Must Overcome When Flipping Properties

To read most of the property-flipping books, you would think that flipping a piece of property is as easy as changing clothes. I hate to be a spoil sport, but in reality nothing could be further from the truth. The fact of the matter is that most authors fail to point out the potential deal-killing obstacles that investors must overcome when using conventional property-flipping strategies. And they never bother to mention anything about:

1. Title seasoning.
2. Loan seasoning.
3. Property appraisals.
4. Overzealous scrutiny from lenders and title and escrow agents for possible fraud.
5. Stringent financial tests, which investors must pass in order to qualify for a mortgage or deed of trust loan on a non-owner-occupied property.

I can tell you from firsthand observations that most of the investors who try their hand at flipping properties usually end up spinning their wheels. While I was writing this chapter, I received a telephone call from an investor here in Tampa who wanted to know if I was interested in buying a small commercial property that he had under contract to purchase. As I found out, this guy was unable to finance the purchase of the property, and his purchase agreement was due to expire in five days. He was in a panic mode, frantically trying to find someone to buy his agreement before he lost his earnest money deposit and the seller filed a lawsuit against him for failing to purchase the property as agreed. I passed on the deal but took down the property's street address for future reference. Who knows, if the property fits my needs, I may contact the owner later on and try to negotiate an option to purchase.

Six Costs That Eat Up Profits When Flipping Properties

The main reason I cannot get excited about the property-flipping strategies that are being taught today is that they are way too expensive. There are six costs involved in flipping a property that eat up profits just like a Florida sinkhole sucks up fill dirt:

1. Acquisition costs.
2. Transaction costs.
3. Closing costs.
4. Repair costs.
5. Holding costs.
6. Sales costs.

The truth of the matter is that investors have no real control over how much a property-flipping transaction will ultimately cost them. The reason for this lack of cost control is that the actual amount of the holding cost is unknown when flipping a property. Holding costs include debt service, insurance, property taxes, maintenance, and security. And the single largest cost of holding on to a piece of property is its debt service or monthly loan payments. The problem with being the proud owner of a piece of investment property is that the mortgage meter is always running, whether the property is occupied or vacant. I learned this lesson the hard way when a property-flipping deal, which I thought was going to be a slam-dunk, turned out to be an air ball instead. When I was young and dumb, I bought a run-down single-family house in South Tampa with the intent of turning it around and reselling it for a fast profit. In those days, the term *flip* was not widely used. I quickly fixed up the house and put it up for sale at a below-market purchase price and waited for the thundering herd of buyers. Well, after six months and $3,800 in mortgage payments, I sold my money pit for a whopping $4,500 profit! This is when I decided there had to be a better way, and I started to learn about real estate options. I came to the realization that it would be much cheaper, easier, and faster to flip a real estate option than a piece of property.

Why the Concurrent Closing Strategy Is Usually Extremely Hard to Implement

Another popular property-flipping strategy that is being taught today is *concurrent closings,* which are better known as *simultaneous closings, double closings,* and *double escrows.* Under a typical concurrent closing scenario, Buyer A signs a purchase agreement to buy a property from Seller B; in the meantime, Buyer A turns around and signs a purchase agreement to sell the property to Buyer C at the same time Buyer A buys the property from Seller B. In theory, this sounds as easy as boiling water, but in reality, it is next to impossible to pull off, especially when there are lenders involved in the transaction, because, nowadays, almost all lenders issue closing instructions to title and escrow agents doing concurrent closings, which require:

1. *The source of title:* The source of title gives the name, date, and recording information of the document that transferred the property's title to the current owner.
2. *The source of funds:* The source of funds provides information on where the money came from to purchase the property. This is done to prevent the end buyer from funding the seller's purchase of the property from the original owner. In other words, each transaction within the concurrent closing must be funded by each buyer.
3. *Full disclosure:* All three parties involved in the two separate transactions must be made aware of one another.
4. *HUD 1 Settlement Statements:* Properly completed HUD 1 Settlement Statements, which accurately document all of the payments made in each transaction and match the actual checks that were disbursed during each closing.

A major flaw in the concurrent closing strategy is that it is illegal to sell any property to which you do not own the title. In legal circles, this is commonly referred to as *grand theft*. For example, in 2002, the Florida Bar Association disciplined an attorney (Florida Supreme Court Case No. SC01-2321) for acting as legal counsel and the closing agent in a real estate transaction involving selling property the attorney's client did not legally own. The attorney and his client were arrested and charged with grand theft, organized fraud, and obtaining a mortgage or promissory note by false representation. The attorney had participated in a so-called double closing, which he later claimed he did not know was illegal, during which his client closed on a contract to sell a property prior to closing on the contract to purchase the same property. Thus, at the time of the closing on the sales contract, the attorney's client did not own the property because the closing with the original, legitimate seller had not yet taken place. In other words, the attorney knowingly participated in a transaction in which his client sold property to a third party, to which the client did not own the title. However, all of these legal problems could have been avoided if the attorney had advised his client to buy a real estate option instead of the property!

Why It Makes More Financial Sense to Flip Options instead of Properties

In the first part of this chapter, I gave you the lowdown on why most of the property-flipping strategies being taught today are too expensive and hard to implement. Now, I tell you why real estate options are less risky, more profitable, and easier to use than 99 percent of all the property-flipping strategies being peddled today. I also tell you why it makes more financial sense to flip real estate options instead of properties. First off, when you buy an option rather than a property, you are not going to be saddled with the financial responsibilities that go along with outright property ownership. And you are not going to get stuck paying any of the costs that are involved in a typical property-flipping transaction. Plus, you will not have to jump through any flaming financial hoops in order to get some lender to give you a mortgage or deed of trust loan. You will never have to worry about being sued by a seller because you failed to close on the purchase of a property. But most importantly, when you flip an option, instead of a property, you do not need to worry about having title or escrow agents looking over your shoulder and checking to see if your deal meets with their approval. As you will learn in Chapter 19, when you flip or sell an option agreement to a third party, all you have to do is complete and sign an assignment of real estate option agreement and collect the assignment fee, and it is a done deal. And then it is off to the bank to cash your check!

I know an investor who specializes in buying options on properties that have been used as methamphetamine labs. His only buying criterion is that the property must be located within a 100-mile radius of Tampa. This guy is a real professional, who can turn a contaminated property around in 15 days or less. And just as soon as a property is cleaned up and certified as being fit for human habitation, he sells his option to another investor, who exercises the option and buys the property. This guy claims to be doing between 12 and 15 deals a year, with an average profit of $8,500 per property.

Savvy Investors Can Use Real Estate Options to Provide Just-in-Time Property

Last, one of the things that I like most about real estate options is that I can use them to provide just-in-time (JIT) property. *Just-in-time inventory management* refers to the practice of ordering an inventory of parts or raw materials on an as-needed basis, versus maintaining a large on-hand inventory. The automotive industry in the United States has used JIT inventory management for over a decade. Today, savvy real estate investors can apply the same JIT inventory management principles when using real estate options. All they need to do is to find a particular type of property that is in demand in their local real estate market and then use a real estate option to gain control of a piece of property that fits the bill. Then they flip the option to an end user or buyer who has a need for the property.

CHAPTER 2

The Most Profitable
Types of Properties to Buy
Real Estate Options On

You need to know right from the get-go that, as a real estate option investor, you are not going to have option property deals served up to you on a silver platter by eager sellers and real estate brokers. In this business, the most profitable option deals are usually the ones that investors create from scratch by identifying an unfulfilled need in their local real estate market and putting a property under option, which best fills the need, and then reselling the option to a buyer, who has a use for the property. And unlike conventional real estate transactions, which usually involve properties that have been heavily advertised over a period of time, the most profitable types of properties to buy options on are not generally advertised as being for sale. Instead, they are bought through what is known in the real estate trade as an unsolicited offer to purchase. The best types of option properties are not for sale or listed with real estate brokers because they are vacant and in a dirty, neglected, run-down condition. The problem with properties that are in what most people consider to be an unmarketable condition is that they are hard to sell and even harder to finance. In most cases, property owners do not have the time and money to put their property into a marketable condition. But even if an owner did want to get his or her property in tiptop shape, it would be next to impossible to get a lender to finance the fix-up on reasonable terms. And unless a buyer has deep pockets or a sugar daddy willing to cosign the loan, conventional lenders generally shy away from financing the purchase of vacant, run-down, non-income-producing properties. The only sources of loans to finance the purchase of vacant properties in a dilapidated condition are hard money lenders, who usually charge outrageous loan fees and the maximum interest rate allowed by law. The fact of the matter is that vacant properties in dire need of repairs that most lenders are unwilling to finance are not exactly the type of properties that most real estate brokers are looking to list for sale. Nowadays, most brokers will not touch a property like that with a 10-foot pole. They are looking for the easy-to-sell properties in turnkey condition that appeal to most prospective buyers.

Not All Properties Are Option Properties

Vilfredo Pareto was an Italian economist who lived from 1848 to 1923. Pareto observed that 20 percent of the Italian people owned 80 percent of the nation's accumulated wealth. Pareto's observation became known as the *Pareto Principle*. Today, the Pareto Principle is commonly referred to as the 80/20 rule. This 80/20 rule is based on the principle that 80 percent of all results are derived from 20 percent of all effort. This means that 80 percent of all activity is a lesson in futility and wasted effort. The 80/20 rule, as it applies to buying real estate options, can be best summed up in this corollary: Eighty percent of all real estate option profits come from just 20 percent of all properties. In other words, 8 out of every 10 properties are not potential option properties. But there is no such thing as a perfect option property. As you will learn in this chapter, the most profitable types of properties to put under option are usually castoffs and dysfunctional properties—what I commonly refer to as bad buildings—with hidden profit potential, which is not visible to most real estate investors.

Best to Include a Worst-Case Scenario in Your Option Buying Decision Process

The very last step in my option buying decision-making process is to develop a worst-case scenario for the property under consideration. I do this because I am a pragmatic realist, and I fully understand that there is always a fifty-fifty chance that something could happen during the option period that could prevent me from reselling my option to a third party. And this is why the very first question that I always ask myself when I have a property under serious consideration is this: What is the absolute worst thing that could go wrong after I buy an option on this property, and could I survive it financially? In most cases, the worst-case scenario is that the property could be foreclosed on, come under the control of a federal bankruptcy court trustee, or be forfeited to a government agency, or I will not able to sell my option before it expires. In cases like these, the worst that can happen is that I end up losing my option fee. Granted, this is not something that I relish, but I could survive it financially. However, if I came up with a financially devastating worst-case scenario for a potential option property that had a much better than fifty-fifty chance of occurring, I would pass on the property. And I suggest that you do the same!

You Must Be Able to Visualize a Property Being Put to a Variety of Uses

One of the keys to consistently making money as a real estate option investor is the ability to look at a piece of vacant property and visualize it being put to a variety of profitable uses. The real estate buzzword for this is *adaptive reuse,* which refers to putting a property to use in a way in which it was not originally intended. For example, when most people look at a vacant three-bay gas station, all they ever see is just a vacant three-bay gas station. However, when a savvy real estate option investor with a fertile imagination looks at a vacant three-bay gas station, he or she immediately sees a:

1. Produce market.
2. Convenience store.
3. Tool rental store.
4. Pizza parlor.
5. Plant nursery.
6. Small engine repair shop.
7. Set of small office suites.
8. Delicatessen.

To illustrate my point, I once paid $3,000 for a six-month option on a condemned mom and pop-type convenience store in East Tampa, which had been involved in a fire. However, the building was structurally sound and the roof was still intact, as most of the actual fire damage had been confined to the shelving, coolers, and contents of the store. The person operating the store was uninsured, so the fire wiped out his business. And after I had an opportunity to carefully inspect the property, I no longer saw a burnt-out convenience store; instead, I saw a thriving produce market, and that is exactly how I packaged the property. To spiff up the property, I gave the exterior an industrial-strength cleaning and had the interior of the store gutted and cleaned out, so that would-be produce mavens could walk around inside and visualize where they could place their various fruits and vegetables. Two months later, I turned around and resold my option to a hard-working Korean family for an $18,000 profit.

Read Various Trade Publications
to Help Find Deals

The ability to visualize a property being put to other uses is a skill that you can quickly develop by expanding your knowledge of the types of properties that house various businesses and industries. I read over 20 trade publications a month, which cover a variety of industries, ranging from transportation to logistics to site selection to metal building construction to operating convenience stores. The one thing that all of these trade publications have in common is that they are all involved in real estate in one form or the other. I read these magazines, which, by the way, I receive free of charge, to help stimulate my creative thought process about the various ways in which a piece of property can be put to use. And this helps me to connect the dots between a particular type of property that is in demand and the prospective buyers who may have an urgent need for that type of property. I am also able to pick up bits and pieces of information about the real estate needs of various types of businesses and industries throughout the southeastern United States. For example, a couple of years ago, I read a property wanted ad in a trade publication where a national convenience store chain was seeking a 10,000 square foot refrigerated warehouse in Central Florida, between Tampa and Orlando. I called the person in charge of the real estate department to see if the company would be interested in purchasing an existing warehouse, which could be converted into a cold storage facility. She said they would if the purchase price came in below the replacement cost for an existing facility and the property was located in Lakeland, Florida. I called my insurance broker, who gave me the current cost per square foot to replace a refrigerated warehouse in Lakeland, which is located in Polk County, right smack dab in the middle between Tampa and Orlando. I immediately called the Polk County Property Appraiser's Office and ordered a listing on CD-ROM of all the parcels in Polk County under code number 48 of the Florida Department of Revenue's land use code, which is used to designate warehouses and distribution centers. In my property data request to the property appraiser, I asked for the parcel address, assessed value, square footage, and type of construction, along with the owner's mailing address. Once I received the list, which cost me a grand total of $60, I deleted every parcel with a building over 15,000 square feet from the CD-ROM. Next, I deleted all of the parcels that did not have buildings made of concrete block construction. I wanted concrete block buildings because they provide better insulation than metal or wood, which is important in a hot place like Florida. I ended up with a list of 12 properties that met my basic criteria. I looked up the properties on the property appraiser's web site and then did a quick drive-by inspection of each property. Out of the 12 properties, three were run-down and appeared to be vacant. And those were the three property owners that I sent letters to, proposing to buy a one-year option. I ended up buying an option on one of the properties for $5,000, which I resold a month later to the convenience store chain for a $25,000 profit. All in all, I had spent less than 40 hours putting the whole deal together. However, I would never have had a $25,000 payday if I had not read the property wanted ad in a trade publication and then been able to connect the dots!

Your Option Buying Decisions Should Include Local Property Supply and Demand

One surefire way to quickly go out of business as a real estate option investor is to buy options on properties that are not in demand in your local real estate market. If you are smart, you will follow my advice and use the information that is readily available on local economic, business, and real estate market conditions to help you determine which types of properties to buy options on. This way, you will be able to make an informed option buying decision, which is based on the local supply and demand for a particular type of property. You can stay informed of local market conditions by:

1. Reading local business and real estate-related publications.
2. Logging on to local college, chamber of commerce, business, and real estate-related web sites.
3. Listening to and watching local business and real estate-related news broadcasts.
4. Attending networking functions with local business and real estate professionals.

But in addition to considering local property supply and demand, you need to develop your own real estate option property selection criteria, which are compatible with your personal interests, finances, and available time. This way, you can focus on a specific type of property and not waste your time, money, and energy pursuing properties in a willy-nilly fashion. Your option property selection criteria should include the:

1. Types of properties you are interested in buying options on.
2. Property price range that you can afford to invest in.
3. Percentage of the purchase price that you can afford to pay for an option.
4. Geographical areas that you feel comfortable investing in.

Why It's Best to Specialize in at Least Two Different Types of Option Properties

How many different types of option properties you specialize in pretty much depends on the size of your local real estate market. At a minimum, I recommend that you specialize in at least two different types of properties. I am telling you this because in most real estate markets, very few potentially profitable option properties are usually available. And if you focus on just one type of property, you probably will not be very successful. The most profitable option investors that I know specialize in at least two different types of option properties. For example, I know one investor who buys options on single-family houses that have been damaged by sinkholes. This same investor—as I mentioned in Chapter 1—also buys options on single-family houses and mobile homes that have been used as laboratories for producing illegal methamphetamine drugs. I know another option investor who specializes in buying options on building lots with condemned single-family houses, which have been slated for demolition. He also buys single-family houses that have been repeatedly cited for major health code violations, caused by too many pet animals residing in the property over a long period of time. My two favorite types of properties to buy real estate options on are:

1. Small, vacant, filthy, run-down commercial properties.
2. Condemned single-family houses, which are located in emerging commercial areas and can be easily, quickly, and inexpensively rezoned for commercial use.

The Seven Most Profitable Types of Properties to Buy Options On

The real trick to being a successful option investor is in knowing which properties to put under option so that you can create instant equity without having to spend oodles of time and gobs of money on an extreme property makeover. And over the years, I have been able to take the same derelict properties, which most uninformed investors reject out of hand as being hopeless cases, and by using just a smidgen of imagination and some old-fashioned creative thinking, I have turned them into profitable option properties. From my experiences, the seven most profitable types of properties to buy real estate options on are:

1. Properties that can be rezoned for more profitable uses.
2. Small mismanaged rental properties that can be turned around.

3. Properties condemned for demolition because of code violations.
4. Dirty, filthy, run-down properties that can be cleaned up.
5. Properties with correctable problems that make them non-marketable.
6. Properties that have been stigmatized.
7. Properties with obsolescent flaws that can be put to other uses.

What the preceding seven types of properties have in common is that they are all well below the radar screens of the so-called big guy investors, such as publicly traded real estate investment companies, and they usually:

1. Belong to absentee owners.
2. Are in a filthy, neglected, run-down condition.
3. Have flaws that make them non-marketable.
4. Are not being put to their most profitable use.
5. Can be bought at prices at least 20 percent below their current market value.
6. Have immediate resale profit potential when marketed to a targeted group of prospective buyers.

In most real estate markets nationwide, savvy, knowledgeable real estate option investors who really know what they are doing have very little real competition from other individual real estate investors for these types of properties. This is because the average real estate investor is not very sophisticated when it comes to putting relatively complex deals together. Plus, they are generally intimidated by any property other than a single-family house or duplex and are reluctant to make offers on properties that are not for sale by the owner or listed with a broker.

Properties That Can Be Rezoned for More Profitable Uses

A lucrative option strategy is to buy options on properties that can be easily re-zoned for more profitable uses. Easily rezoned properties are those well below the public radar screen and not located close to neighborhoods that are inhabited by vocal activists who make it a habit to protest all zoning requests at public zoning hearings. In other words, do not buy an option on a single-family house in a tranquil residential neighborhood and expect to get a rezoning request for an "adult business" approved. The best types of property to use this strategy on are single-family houses in emerging commercial areas where similar rezoning requests have been recently approved. This strategy is covered in Chapter 7. Keep in mind that a single-family house that can be rezoned for use as a professional office has a lot more profit potential than a house that can be used only as a residential property because the monthly rental rate for a professional office is much higher than the rental rate for a single-family house. And the value of a piece of income-producing property is determined by the annual amount of rental income the property generates—the higher the income, the higher the resale value. When you look at a property with rezoning in mind, you must always ask yourself the following three questions:

Question 1: What is the most profitable use for this property?

Question 2: Is there sufficient demand for the most profitable use of this property?

Question 3: Can this property be rezoned for its most profitable use?

Small Mismanaged Rental Properties That Can Be Turned Around

Another profitable type of property to buy options on is small mismanaged rental properties that:

1. Are located in stable, low-crime, moderate-income neighborhoods that are within close proximity to large employers, military bases, schools, shopping centers, and healthcare facilities.
2. Have below-market rental rates, which can be increased by at least $150 per rental unit once the property turnaround has been completed.
3. Have mismanagement problems that can be quickly and inexpensively corrected by implementing aggressive professional property management practices.
4. Are structurally sound and have deferred maintenance that can be quickly and inexpensively repaired.
5. Can be bought for at least 20 percent below market value on buyer-friendly terms with seller-financed mortgage or deed of trust loans.

My company, Home Equities Corp, specializes in small (2- to 12-unit) mismanaged rental properties that can be quickly turned around by giving the property a cosmetic facelift and implementing aggressive professional property management practices. This strategy is covered in detail in Chapter 8.

Properties Cited for Code Violations

One of the biggest problems that vacant property owners face is vandalism, and vandals have a tendency to create unsightly properties, which generate a flood of complaint calls to local code enforcement departments. Once this happens and the property is cited for code violations, it must be brought into compliance—usually within 30 to 60 days—or the owner will face having to pay a daily fine until all of the cited repairs are completed. And if the owner does absolutely nothing, the property will end up being condemned by the bureaucrats down at city hall for building, health and safety, and fire code violations. When this sequence of events occurs, the property usually becomes a bona fide problem property, the kind I like to buy real estate options on!

Finding a Niche in "Dirty Deals"

One of my favorite types of property to buy real estate options on are small, vacant, filthy, run-down commercial properties, which can be quickly and inexpensively cleaned up. I have found my own little niche in what I call "dirty deals." Dirty deals are small, vacant commercial buildings that are structurally sound, but have a filthy, neglected, run-down appearance, which is an instant turnoff to most people who cannot see beyond the filth and grime. The reason I like these dirty deals so much is that they are strictly cleaner-upper properties that do not require an extreme makeover. All I have to do to spruce them up is give them an old-fashioned industrial-strength cleaning. This way, I do not have any of my own money tied up in costly and time-consuming repairs. My out-of-pocket expenses are limited to the cost of cleaning up the property. I like this particular type of property because I can usually buy real estate options on them at bargain basement prices and then quickly resell the option for a hefty profit once the property has been given an industrial-strength cleaning.

I once bought a real estate option on a filthy, neglected, run-down, but structurally sound house in a so-called neighborhood-in-transition in Winter Park, Florida, a suburb of Orlando. The house had been condemned for building, safety, health, and fire code violations. This place looked like something right out of downtown Baghdad, Iraq! It had what code enforcement inspectors commonly refer to as accumulations of every type of debris, garbage, and junk known to mankind! The owner lived in Westerville, Ohio, and wanted the steady stream of threatening letters from the Winter Park Code Enforcement Board to stop. I had done my homework and knew the property was worth at least $110,000 after it was cleaned up. I ended up paying $500 for a six-month option to purchase the house for $75,000. It cost me $2,000 and took three days to have all of the accumulations removed from the property and have the house, driveway, and walkways pressure washed. Three weeks later, I turned around and resold my real estate option for a $15,000 profit!

Properties with Correctable Problems

To me, a problem property is any property, or owner, experiencing any of the following types of problems, which can be corrected:

1. Title problems.
2. Ownership problems.
3. Management problems.
4. Vacancy problems.
5. Financial problems.
6. Maintenance problems.
7. Tenant problems.
8. Cash flow problems.
9. Structural problems.
10. Code violation problems.

Stigmatized Properties

The National Association of Realtors defines a *stigmatized property* as: "a property that has been psychologically impacted by an event, which occurred or was suspected to have occurred on the property, such event being one that has no physical impact of any kind." Most stigmatized properties are in flawless physical condition, but have become tainted because they were the site of murders, HIV-related deaths, rapes, suicides, robberies, kidnappings, child molestations, and accidental deaths, or are believed to be haunted by ghosts. These are examples of intangible or psychological stigmas, which are based on individual personal perceptions. However, tangible or real stigmas can be the result of a property being located in an area:

1. Known for building defects.
2. Infested with gangs of criminals.
3. Next to a halfway house for soon-to-be-released criminals.
4. Bordering a group home for sex offenders.
5. Close to hazardous waste material.

6. Near a landfill, slaughterhouse, pig farm, sewage treatment plant, or other nuisance-type property.

Because of their history, stigmatized properties often scare away prospective buyers, who are worried about decreases in property values and marketability. Today, many states have stigmatized property statutes, which require property owners to disclose certain types of stigmas that are part of a property's history.

Obsolescent Properties That Can Be Put to Profitable Use

Thanks in large part to rapidly changing technology, there are vacant commercial and industrial properties in just about every real estate market nationwide that have outlived their original use and have been labeled as being functionally obsolescent properties. However, the vast majority of these so-called obsolescent properties are not ready for the wrecking ball. Many are structurally sound buildings that are relatively new and have many years of use left in them. In Chapter 4, you get the lowdown on how you can make money from obsolescent properties that can be put to more profitable uses.

CHAPTER 3

What It Takes to Be a Profitable Real Estate Option Investor

Before you start reading about the five money-making option strategies, which I have outlined in Part Two of this book, I will tell you what it takes to be a profitable real estate option investor in today's competitive real estate market. In the first part of this chapter, you are going to learn about the traits that separate profitable option investors from the also-rans and wannabes. You do not need to be a card-carrying member of Mensa International, the so-called high IQ society, to make money with options. But you do need to know how to think on your feet and to connect all of the dots so that you can complete a profitable option transaction from scratch and overcome any of the potential deal-killing hurdles, which can pop up at any time. To make it in this business, an investor must possess:

1. A positive mental attitude.
2. An imaginative, analytical, and creative mind.
3. A heavy dose of good old-fashioned common sense.
4. Dogged determination and persistence.
5. Self-confidence and courage.
6. Self-discipline.

A Positive Mental Attitude Is the Most Essential Element in Achieving Success

A positive mental attitude is the most essential element in achieving lasting success in any type of worthwhile endeavor. And from my observations, the people with a real can-do attitude are the ones who generally get ahead in life. The following inspirational quotation from author Walter D. Wintle best sums up the power of a positive mental attitude:

> If you think you are beaten, you are. If you think you dare not, you don't. If you like to win, but you think you can't, it's almost a cinch you won't. If you think you'll lose, you've lost. For out in the world we find success begins with a fellow's will. It's all in the state of mind. If you think you are outclassed, you are. You've got to be sure of yourself before you can ever win a prize. Life's battles don't always go to the stronger or faster man, but sooner or later the man who wins is the one who thinks he can ("The Man Who Thinks He Can," *Respectfully Quoted: Dictionary of Quotations,* 1989).
>
> And if you happen to be one of the many people in America who have an overly negative attitude, you are in desperate need of what is known in the Marine Corps as an attitude adjustment. In simple terms, an attitude adjustment involves changing or adjusting your outlook on life, from that of a skeptical pessimist looking for nothing but the worst, to an open-minded optimist, who focuses on the reward instead of the risk. This does not mean that you ignore risks; it simply means that you no longer let them stop you from achieving success.

Don't Let Your Fear of Failure Stop You from Being a Profitable Option Investor

First off, all rational, reasonable, intelligent adults have an innate fear of failure. In fact, most Americans are continually warned from birth to be careful and watch out for the unforeseen. However, it is how human beings are able to overcome the very real fear of failure that determines whether an individual will eventually be successful in a given endeavor. I use my own fear of failure to keep me motivated when I am in the middle of a project. So, if fear of failure is what you feel is holding you back from becoming a profitable option investor, I have a possible solution that just might work. I am usually not a big fan of what I refer to as the rah, rah crowd—so-called motivational speakers—because I believe that lasting motivation is something that comes from within. However, I highly recommend that you listen to the following two audio programs by best-selling author Earl Nightingale: *The Strangest Secret in the World for Succeeding Today* and *Lead the Field,* which are available at the following Nightingale-Conant web site: www.nightingale.com.

Avoid Listening to the Naysayers Who Tell You That It Can't Be Done

Please, whatever you do, do not be swayed from your dreams by the naysayers who tell you that what you are proposing cannot be done. If I had listened to all of the naysayers throughout my life, I would probably be living in a cardboard box under an overpass in Bugtussle, New Hampshire. But luckily for me, I was too dumb at the time to know that my ideas would not work. As far as I am concerned, one of the very worst things that any person can do is to make financial and business decisions based solely on the advice of ignorant people who have never accomplished anything worthwhile in their entire adult lives! Yet, that is exactly what happens thousands of times a day all across America. Bright, ambitious people full of pep and vinegar listen to overly skeptical cynics, who repeatedly tell them that it cannot be done, and then they, too, believe that it cannot be done and end up doing nothing. So please do yourself a huge favor and stop listening to the world-class skeptics in your life, who are most likely immediate family members such as good old mom and dad, along with Brother Bob, Sister Sue, and Uncle Elmo, and close, personal friends. And I am not telling you to disown the naysayers in your life; I am just asking you to stop listening to them!

Twenty Reasons Most People Fail to Make It as Real Estate Investors

As an author, I always strive to tell it to my readers as it really is. I do not believe in sugarcoating the truth. And that is why I want you to know that most people—more than 51 percent—fail miserably as real estate investors. I am telling you this not to discourage you, but to warn you about the consequences of investing in real estate in a haphazard manner. I attribute this relatively high failure rate to the fact that the real estate investment business does not have any of the so-called barriers to entry, which many other businesses have. In other words, there are no background, educational, competency-testing, licensing, insurance, or capital requirements to set up shop as a real estate investor. Anyone can enter the business at any time, without the slightest clue as to how to operate a profitable real estate investment business. As a result, most people usually fail to make it as real estate investors for one or more of the following reasons:

Reason 1:   Paying above market value for property.

Reason 2:   Lack of persistence.

Reason 3:   Lack of organizational skills.

Reason 4:   Lack of local real estate market knowledge.

Reason 5:   Inability to stay focused on a single objective.

Reason 6:   Failure to act in a timely manner.

Reason 7:   No clearly defined exit strategy.

Reason 8:   Lack of capital and credit.

Reason 9:   Lack of clearly defined investment goals.

Reason 10:   Unrealistic expectations.

Reason 11:   Bad advice from unreliable sources.

Reason 12:   Lack of planning.

Reason 13:   Poor record keeping.

Reason 14:   Lack of self-discipline.

Reason 15:   Lack of basic real estate investment knowledge.

Reason 16:   Lack of patience.

Reason 17:   Lack of mental toughness.

Reason 18:   Inability to manage time.

Reason 19:   Failure to perform adequate due diligence inspections.

Reason 20:   Failure to prioritize tasks in accordance with their importance.

Real Estate Options Are Not for Dummies

As I alluded to in the introduction to this chapter, real estate options are definitely not for dummies. To make it as a profitable option investor, you need to possess an imaginative, analytical, and creative mind. First, you must have the imagination to be able to visualize various types of properties being put to a myriad of different uses. And then you must be able to put an option deal together from scratch that makes financial sense to all of the parties involved in the transaction. Finally, you must be creative enough to package the property for maximum resale value and market it to a targeted group of prospective buyers who are willing to pay your asking price. Granted, this is not rocket science, but you will not get very far as an option investor if you have no imagination, cannot solve problems, and have zero creativity. Nowadays, too many people fall into the trap of mistaking education for brains. I know of a certain Harvard Business School graduate who flaunts his MBA degree every chance he gets, yet he has pretty much been a flop as a real estate investor. He apparently does not have the temperament and mental toughness and just cannot hack it in real estate. On the other hand, one of the sharpest real estate minds that I have ever encountered belongs to a 25-year-old high school dropout with only a GED or high school equivalency diploma. The thing that this real estate whiz kid has over most other people who are better educated is that he is constantly thinking two moves ahead of the other party in a transaction. And he has an abundance of good old-fashioned common sense. In other words, he has the good sense to know that when you buy an option on a piece of property, you are also buying an option on the property's location. So, he never gets sucked into buying an option on the best property in a bad area.

Don't Give Up and Quit before You Achieve Your Objective

Americans today live in a drive-in society where just about everything under the sun is available from the front seat of an automobile. And as a nation, we are the most impatient people on the planet. When we want something, we want it right now, instantaneously. Well, that type of impatient attitude may be hunky-dory when it comes to customers' expectations about the service at fast-food restaurants, but it will not fly when applied to the real estate option business. Being a profitable option investor requires consistent persistence and dogged determination, which prevents investors from quitting the first time things do not go exactly as planned. Trust me, the only thing that you can depend on in this business is that things will almost never go the way you think they should. And in a way, I suppose that is a good thing because if options were a piece of cake, everyone would be using them, and that would be bad for business. So, if you are looking for some magic formula that will tell you how to make a million bucks with real estate options by next Thursday, you are reading the wrong book. You must understand that the real estate option strategies that I have outlined in this book will work only if you do. In other words, if you really want to be a profitable option investor, you must first be willing to get up off your dead duff and put in the time and effort necessary to fully understand the information that is contained in this book. And then, you must be willing to go beyond where most people fear to tread and actually put what you have learned to practical use. Anything else is a colossal waste of time!

You Do Not Need a Big Checkbook to Become an Option Investor

One of the main reasons real estate options appeal to so many people is that you do not need a six-figure income, a hefty bank account, an 850 FICO score. The term FICO refers to the name of the company, Fair Isaac Corporation, that developed the popular credit scoring model named FICO, and a lifetime employment contract in order to become an option investor. The fact of the matter is that buyers of options usually face very little financial scrutiny. For example, when buying an option, you almost always avoid having to pass any of the financial tests—income, debt, and credit scoring—that are such an integral part of the buying process. This is mainly because many property owners involved in an option transaction seem to focus only on the amount of the option fee they will receive from the deal and pay scant attention to the party buying the option. The only financial test that most people must pass when buying a real estate option is having the cash necessary to pay the option consideration fee. The amount of money that you will need to do your first option deal depends on what segment of your local real estate market you target. For example, my target market in Hillsborough County, Florida, is commercial properties up to $500,000 in value. Please keep in mind that a commercial property that sells for $500,000 in Tampa would cost double that amount in the Northeast and triple that price in California. And depending on the property's condition and the owner's circumstances, it usually costs me between $5,000 and $15,000 to buy a six-month to one-year option. My only out-of-pocket expenses are the costs of cleaning up and marketing the property, which typically run between $2,500 and $4,500 per deal. How much startup capital you will need to get into the option business pretty much depends on your local real estate market and the price of the properties you pursue. I know an investor in Phoenix, Arizona, who paid only $500 for a six-month option on a vacant single-family house, which belonged to an absentee owner residing in Riverside, California. And just 30 days later, she flipped her option to an investor from Los Angeles for a nice $10,000 profit. Next, she invested $1,500 of her profits into a one-year option on a run-down duplex, which she resold 90 days later for a $12,000 profit. On her first two deals, she leveraged $2,000 into a $22,000 profit without ever having to buy any property. As far as raising startup capital to get your business off the ground, your best bets are:

1. Fixed-rate, low-interest lines of unsecured credit.
2. Home equity loans.

Use Fixed-Rate, Low-Interest Lines of Unsecured Credit to Buy Options

I use fixed-rate, low-interest lines of unsecured credit to finance the purchase of options. *Unsecured lines of credit* are issued through unsecured credit cards. I currently use two $40,000 lines of unsecured credit, which have fixed-interest rates of between 3.4 percent and 4.5 percent. I am able to obtain these low-rate lines of unsecured credit because I have zero consumer debt and a credit score in the top 5 percent. The real beauty in using unsecured lines of credit, instead of secured credit lines such as a home equity line of credit (HELOC), is that you do not have to put your home on the line and pay those exorbitant closing costs that lenders generally charge borrowers for the privilege of doing business with them. In fact, the most that I have ever had to pay when using an unsecured line of credit was a $50 transfer fee.

Why You Must Use Today's Technology in Your Option Investment Business

First things first: You cannot have a phobia of computers and be successful in this business. To be successful, you must use today's technology in your option investment business. I divide the real estate investment business into Before the Internet (BTI) and After the Internet (ATI). In fact, I consider the Internet to be the great equalizer! I say this because before the Internet became available to the general public, the average individual real estate investor had no way to readily access public property ownership records and a myriad of other essential real estate-related records. Today, anyone with a personal computer and an Internet connection who knows where to look can gain access to the same information that Fortune 500 companies use to make business decisions. Please understand that when I tell you to incorporate today's technology into your business, I do not mean that you should waste your hard-earned money buying the latest gizmos and gadgets on the market—handheld wireless computers, global positioning devices, and digital personal assistants. Do not tie up your available investment capital in a bunch of overpriced equipment, which will not put a single penny in your pocket. However, I do recommend that every serious real estate option investor have a:

1. Late-model personal computer with Microsoft Windows 2000 or newer operating system and Microsoft Word 2000 or newer word processing software.
2. Quality laser printer.
3. Reliable high-speed Internet connection.
4. Reliable cell phone.

You do not need to hock the family jewels to set up shop as an option investor. I am a former New England Yankee who strictly adheres to the use-it-up, make-it-do, wear-it-out, or do-without philosophy that is common throughout northern New England. And my wife, Barbara, and I are both board-certified penny pinchers, who know how to pinch a penny until it screams! We are not cheap; we just do not like to spend our hard-earned money when we do not have to. For example, in my real estate investment business, I use a Compaq 7550 personal computer that I bought at Sam's Club for under $600. My computer came with a Microsoft 2003 Windows XP operating system. I use Microsoft Word 2003 word processing software, which I also picked up at Sam's Club for $245. My laser printer is a Hewlett Packard LaserJet 1300, which I purchased at Sam's Club for under $400. I use a four-year-old Qualcom dual-band cell phone that I bought from Sprint PCS for less than $100. My total equipment cost was right around $1,345, which I wrote off as a business expense for tax purposes. My cell phone bill is less than $40 a month, and I spend under $50 a month for a high-speed cable connection to the Internet through Bright House Networks. And, it costs me $25 a month to have my web site on the Internet. My total monthly fixed operating costs are less than $115. Most Americans spend more than that a month on fast food alone, and all they have to show for their money is a big belly and a cholesterol count that is through the roof. So, for a grand total of $2,725, I have equipped my office and paid my fixed operating costs for a year. That works out to roughly $227 a month when broken down over a 12-month period. Granted, this figure covers only fixed operating costs and does not include advertising and mailing expenses. But they, too, can be controlled by using sound business principles.

How to Set Up a Home Office for Your Option Investment Business

For a home office to qualify as a business deduction for federal tax purposes, it must be used regularly and exclusively for business purposes. For example, if you are a part-time real estate investor and a full-time schoolteacher with a home office that you claim as a real estate investment business expense but you use your office for both your real estate investment business and for grading student papers, your home office deduction would be disallowed if you were ever audited by the Internal Revenue Service (IRS). The IRS would do this because your home office is not being used exclusively for business purposes. The best way to make certain that your home office will pass muster with the IRS is to regularly use the space you are claiming as your home office exclusively as your principal place of business. I comply with the IRS home office use rules by having a home office that is located in a separate building behind our home—approximately 40 steps to walk—and used exclusively for business purposes. For more information on how to deduct your home office as a business expense, read IRS Publication 587, *Business Use of Your Home,* which is available online at the following web page: www.irs.gov/pub/irs-pdf/p587.pdf.

Maintain a Separate Checking Account for Your Real Estate Investment Business

For record keeping and tax purposes, you must maintain a separate checking account for your real estate investment business that you can deposit checks into and pay expenses out of. One of the criteria that the IRS uses to determine whether a business is legitimate and not a sham is bank accounts. A business that claims expenses, losses, and depreciation on federal tax returns but does not maintain a bank checking account is going to be suspect and have a very hard time trying to document expenses if ever questioned or audited by the swell folks at the IRS. And the best method for documenting and recording expenses is to pay them with checks written on your real estate investment business checking account or with a credit card issued in the name of your real estate business. This way, you will not have to worry about confusing personal expenses with business expenses. Plus, working out of one checking account will allow you to easily track expenses on a daily basis. The same holds true for using business credit cards to charge business expenses on. For the past 10 years, my company, Home Equities Corp, has used the American Express Optima Card, now called the Business Management Account, to charge all business expenses. Every three months, the American Express Company sends me a detailed quarterly expense statement that is broken down into various categories. This helps to simplify my record keeping and tax preparation.

Internal Revenue Service Publications Available Online

IRS forms and publications are available online in PDF format at the following web page: www.irs.gov/formspubs/index.html.

The following IRS publications pertain to running a real estate investment business:

1. Publication 334, *Tax Guide For Small Business.*
2. Publication 535, *Business Expenses.*

3. Publication 583, *Starting a Business and Keeping Records.*
4. Publication 587, *Business Use of Your Home.*
5. Publication 1779, *Independent Contractor or Employee.*

Don't Run Out and Form a Separate Business Entity before You Do Any Deals

Do not make the all-too-common mistake of running out and forming a separate business entity before you have done any option deals. As far as I am concerned, it is totally asinine for aspiring option investors to go to the effort and expense of forming a separate business entity solely for the purpose of buying options before they even know if they are cut out to be an option investor. However, to those of you reading this book who do go on to become profitable option investors, I very highly recommend that you form a separate business entity such as a Subchapter S corporation or limited liability company to buy options through. It is one of the best and least expensive methods available to help reduce your risk and limit your personal liability as a real estate investor. This way, there is a clear distinction between your personal and family assets and the assets held by your corporation or limited liability company. And, in most cases, any liability incurred by the business entity would be limited to the business entity's assets. However, please be advised that there is not a business entity known to man that will protect its owners and officers from being held liable when it's used to engage in fraudulent or criminal behavior. You can find out the filing requirements and fees for forming a business entity in your state by logging on to your state secretary of state's web site and clicking on the division of corporations or a similar name.

Use the Thomaslucier.com Web Site as the Companion Resource for This Book

I recommend that you use my web site, www.thomaslucier.com, as the companion resource for this book. My web site has direct links to all of the web site URLs that are listed throughout this book. There are also direct links to real estate news sources and trade publications. You can also log on to the Question & Answer Forum and e-mail me any questions that you may have about the contents of this book and get a response back within 24 hours. No other real estate book author offers readers this type of one-on-one service!

FIVE REALISTIC STRATEGIES THAT YOU CAN USE TO MAKE MONEY WITH REAL ESTATE OPTIONS TODAY

CHAPTER 4

How You Can Use Options to Make Money from Obsolescent Properties That Can Be Put to More Profitable Uses

The name of the game in this business is to buy options on undervalued properties with immediate resale profit potential. And the only way to maximize a property's profit potential is to put it to its most profitable use. That is why in this chapter I give you the lowdown on how you can use options to control properties that can be put to more profitable uses. Over the past 40 years, the U.S. economy has gone from a manufacturing base to a service and technological base. Today, we live in an age of rapidly changing technology where whole industries can be rendered obsolete overnight. This change in the American economy has resulted in a lot of structurally sound buildings that are functionally obsolete by today's standard, and they are sitting vacant. And most Americans today are caught up in the notion that anything new is automatically better and superior to anything old. So, when people with this mindset come across a property that has been vacant for an extended period of time, they just assume that there must be something wrong with the property. After all, why on earth would a piece of property sit vacant for a long time without attracting any offers to buy it? The truth is that many vacant buildings are relatively new and have a lot of years of use left in them. But we live in a society where people are accustomed to replacing things instead of repairing and reusing them. And this throwaway mentality has carried over into real estate as well. For example, how many times in your own town or city have you seen what appear to be perfectly sound buildings being torn down and replaced when they could have easily been put to another use? As far as I am concerned, this is financial lunacy, when you consider that it is almost always much more cost-effective to buy an existing building that can be adapted for reuse than it is to go out and buy a piece of land and build a brand spanking new building from the ground up. And this is especially true today, given the shortages of building materials and the lack of qualified workers within the construction building trades. The fact of the matter is that when an existing building is put back into use, the property owner avoids all of the rigmarole that is part of the expensive and time-consuming new construction approval and building process, which can include:

1. Opposition from local antigrowth activists.
2. A long drawn-out building approval process.
3. Paying exorbitant building permit and impact fees.
4. Delays caused by shortages of critical building materials and inclement weather conditions.
5. A lack of qualified building contractors.
6. Construction cost overruns that can take years of appreciation in a property's value to recoup.

Definition of an Undervalued
Property with Immediate Resale Profit Potential

For the purpose of buying a real estate option, I define an *undervalued property with immediate resale profit potential* as: "Any property that can be purchased for at least 20 percent below the sale price of comparable properties in similar condition that have sold in the past six months, within a two-mile radius of the potential option property under consideration."

Why Properties with Curable Obsolescent
Flaws Make Ideal Option Properties

Small vacant commercial properties with obsolescent flaws that are economically feasible to cure are potentially the most profitable type of properties to buy real estate options on. I say this because many small, vacant, obsolescent commercial properties:

1. Can often be bought at purchase prices that are below their replacement cost.
2. Have owners who are more willing to sell low-cost real estate options.

3. Are generally off the radar screens of corporate and institutional real estate investors.

4. Scare off most conventional real estate investors.

5. Offer more opportunities to realize immediate resale profits.

Obsolescent Flaws That Cause Properties to Lose Value

The three types of obsolescent flaws that cause properties to lose value are:

1. *Functional obsolescence:* Functional obsolescence occurs when a property loses value due to its architectural design, building style, size, outdated amenities, local economic conditions, and changing technology. Look for properties with design features that would be relatively easy to upgrade or replace. For example, some buildings have facades that include outdated awning-type overhangs that can be removed to give the building a more modern appearance.

2. *Economic obsolescence:* Economic obsolescence occurs when a property loses value because of external factors, such as local traffic pattern changes or the construction of public nuisance-type properties and utilities, such as county jails and sewer treatment plants, on adjoining property. Seek out vacant, but structurally sound, properties that adjoin less desirable nuisance-type properties, for example, a vacant warehouse located next to a sewage treatment plant, which could be used by a manufacturer to store nonhazardous materials.

3. *Physical obsolescence:* Physical obsolescence occurs when a property loses value due to gross mismanagement and physical neglect, resulting in deferred maintenance that is usually too costly to repair. Search for properties with only minor structural problems that can be corrected at a cost that is below the property's replacement cost. In other words, do not buy a real estate option on a property that is deemed to be physically obsolescent if it can be rebuilt from scratch for less than it would cost to repair.

How Commercial Buildings Are Classified

The most profitable types of obsolescent properties to put under option are commercial buildings. The commercial real estate industry classifies commercial buildings according to their location, age, monthly rental rate, amount of amenities, and type of tenants into the following four classes:

1. *Class "A" buildings:* Large, relatively newer buildings with modern amenities such as state-of-the-art telecommunications capability and located in desirable areas.
2. *Class "B" buildings:* Buildings over 10 years old with many amenities that are located in desirable areas.
3. *Class "C" buildings:* Older, well-maintained buildings with smaller size units and fewer amenities and located in stable areas.
4. *Class "D" buildings:* Older buildings with high vacancy rates, deferred maintenance, and very few amenities and located in marginal areas.

Most of the vacant obsolescent properties that I buy options on are Class "C" and "D" buildings, which are located in areas that are on the upswing, but belong to owners who do not have the time, energy, money, or desire to put their obsolescent property to a more profitable use.

How Obsolescent Properties Can Be Put to Their Most Profitable Use

The only reason I invest in real estate instead of widgets is that it is one of the very few businesses left in America where private individual investors can profit handsomely by turning problems into opportunities. And nowadays, white elephant properties can be a bonanza for savvy option investors who have the ability to visualize new lives for buildings that have outlived their original use. In fact, today's real estate lexicon is peppered with buzzwords that are used to describe how obsolescent properties can be put to their most profitable use and includes terms such as:

1. Re-utilization.
2. Conversion.
3. Redevelopment.
4. Recycling.
5. Retrofitting.
6. Repositioning.
7. Revitalization.

And as I told you in Chapter 2, to consistently make money as an option investor, you must develop the ability to look at a piece of vacant property and come up with a variety of viable uses for it—uses that your competitors have overlooked, but which make economic sense. For example, for over two years I drove by a boarded-up gas station located near MacDill Air Force Base in Tampa until one day it dawned on me that this could be an ideal location for a quick oil change and lube shop. I did my market research and found out that the closest oil change shop was 10 miles from the base. And having been in the military, I knew that a lot of service members like to sneak off base during duty hours to run quick errands. To make a long story short, I bought a six-month option for $5,000 and then sent out a detailed property fact sheet, with supporting documentation, to national and regional quick oil change chains. Four months later, I ended up reselling my option to the largest outfit in America for a $25,000 profit!

Why Option Investors Are Usually Buyers of Last Resort for Obsolescent Property

As I told you in Chapter 2, the most profitable type of properties to buy real estate options on are derelict-type properties that do not appeal to many prospective buyers. And they are also the easiest types of property to put under option because option investors are usually buyers of last resort for obsolescent properties. In other words, no one other than an option investor is willing to take a chance on these types of cast-off properties. And when you are the weary owner of a piece of property in less than pristine condition, which has been sitting vacant for a long time with no purchase offers in hand, you cannot be too choosy about how you sell your property. The fact of the matter is that option investors often provide the only hope that the owner of an obsolescent property has of ever selling his or her property. And this lack of demand can put option investors in the driver's seat when it comes to negotiating low-cost option fees and below-market purchase prices on obsolescent properties.

Option Investors Should Focus on Finding New Owners for Obsolescent Properties

When people ask me what I do for a living, I tell them that I am a professional property locator who specializes in using real estate options to control under-valued properties with immediate resale profit potential. I then go on to give a brief explanation of how I go about finding new owners for all types of vacant properties that have outlived their original use but are structurally sound and still have a lot of years left in them before they are ready for the wrecking ball. And this is exactly where your focus should also be when using this strategy to control obsolescent properties. In fact, I have never exercised an option to buy any type of obsolescent property. My approach when using this strategy has always been to locate an obsolescent property, put it under a 6- to 12-month option, market it to a targeted group of prospective buyers, and resell the option. This way, I am able to profit from obsolescent-type properties without the cost, risk, and hassle that go along with actually putting a piece of property to another use. Some of you reading this may think that a professional property locator is nothing more than a glorified bird dog, who receives a finder's fee for locating properties for real estate investors. And you are correct, except for one major difference: An optionee has an exclusive and irrevocable right to purchase the property under option, while the average bird dog has very little or no legal protection to keep investors from bypassing him or her and striking a deal directly with the property owner.

What You Should Check for When Looking Over an Obsolescent Property

When I come across a vacant property with all of the telltale signs of obsolescence that appears to be a potential option property, I always do a quick visual inspection of the outside—I use an inspection checklist like the following sample—to try

---

FORM 4.1   Sample Vacant Property Checklist

---

1. Has the electrical meter been removed from the property? (   ) Yes   (   ) No

2. Is there an electrical power line connected to the property? (   ) Yes   (   ) No

3. Has the property been cited for code violations? (   ) Yes   (   ) No

4. Has the water meter been removed? (   ) Yes   (   ) No

5. Has the property been condemned for demolition? (   ) Yes   (   ) No

6. Is the property infested with termites and rodents? (   ) Yes   (   ) No

7. Are there any visible signs of mold contamination? (   ) Yes   (   ) No

8. Are there any visible signs of environmentally hazardous waste on the property? (   ) Yes   (   ) No

---

to determine just how long the property has been sitting vacant. I need to know this information because I have found that there is usually a direct correlation between how long a property has been vacant and the owner's level of motivation to sell. And it has been my experience that the longer the property has been vacant, the better my chances are of negotiating a low-cost option fee and below-market purchase price.

A word of caution about vacant properties: If there are "No Trespassing" signs posted on the grounds or the outside of a vacant building, do not enter the building. Doing so is not only illegal but also potentially dangerous to your health, especially if the place has been booby-trapped by the owner or occupied by homeless felons. You also risk being mistaken for a burglar and could be shot on sight by the owner. I know an investor here in Tampa who made it a habit of stopping and snooping around the inside of any property, anywhere in the city, that looked the least bit vacant to him. I used to tell him that his curiosity was going to land him in the hospital one day. And lo and behold, one day this real estate sleuth made the near-fatal mistake of opening the front door of what he thought was a vacant house in East Tampa, but which turned out to be the clubhouse of a local street gang. The next thing this guy knew, he was surrounded by a bunch of crack heads wielding aluminum baseball bats, who beat him to within an inch of his life. When I asked him if he was going to be poking around any more vacant properties, he said, "Sure, just as soon as I get my concealed weapon permit." I have a sneaky suspicion that someday he will end up being the lead story on the local six o'clock news, and it will not be about what a swell guy he is! For the record, I do not advise entering a vacant property that you do not own with any type of firearm. To do so, in my opinion, is the epitome of human stupidity and a possible death sentence if the vacant property is occupied by armed criminals who have no compunction whatsoever about pulling the trigger on a handgun or rifle and killing another human being. Now, I do not know about you, but as far as I am concerned, there has not been a property built on this planet that is worth losing my life over, especially a vacant property that I do not even own.

Why You Must Be Able to Think Outside Your Local Real Estate Market

The key to consistently making money with this strategy and every other option strategy that I have outlined in this book is to be able to think outside your own local real estate market. I say this because in my professional opinion, the number one reason that most vacant commercial and industrial properties usually remain vacant for long periods of time is simply that no one in that particular real estate market has been able to come up with a profitable use for the property. And I attribute this to a general lack of vision, creativity, and foresight on the part of most so-called real estate professionals. The fact of the matter is that many of the people involved in real estate today are afflicted with a bad case of tunnel vision, which prevents them from seeing beyond the borders of their own local real estate market. And for whatever reason, they have not been able to apply the marketing concept of buy locally but sell nationally and globally to their real estate investment business. Granted, residential real estate may pretty much be a highly localized business, but that does not mean that the marketing of commercial and industrial real estate should be restricted to the local marketplace. And this is exactly why you must expand your real estate market horizons so that you are able to think outside your local real estate market. To illustrate my point, I recently advised an option investor in Raleigh, North Carolina, who was trying to find a buyer for an option he held on a vacant piece of commercial property, which had been previously used to store replacement parts for large pieces of farm equipment. He had exhausted his list of prospective buyers in the Greater Raleigh Area and did not know which way to turn. I had him e-mail me photos of the interior of the building so that I could see how the interior was laid out. I was especially interested in the distance between support columns and the height of the overhead doors. These two factors are critical to prospective buyers who are looking for a building that can accommodate large trucks or heavy earth-moving equipment, which needs a lot of room to maneuver around inside. It turned out that the building was configured to house big trucks and tractors. Next, I had the investor do a Google search on the Internet to obtain the names and e-mail addresses of everyone within a 500-mile radius of Raleigh who was in any way connected with earth-moving equipment, semi-tractors, and heavy-duty farm equipment. He came up with 50 names and e-mailed each one a property fact sheet, which included photographs of both the exterior and interior of the building. Two months later he resold his option for a $30,000 profit to a company headquartered in Georgia that refurbished earth-moving equipment throughout the Carolinas.

CHAPTER 5

How to Use the Lease and Option Strategy to Make Money with Single-Family Houses

As I told you in the introduction, the straight or naked real estate option strategy that I am writing about in this book is completely different from the so-called lease-option strategy, which has been hailed by numerous lease-option fanatics as the greatest real estate investment strategy since the introduction of nothing down in the late 1970s. But to me, the standard lease-option strategy that is being taught today is just as flawed as the nothing-down strategy of yesteryear! I say this because almost all of the material that has been written on the subject of lease-options glosses over the potential risks, problems, and pitfalls that can occur when using the typical lease-option scheme being peddled today. In fact, the term *lease-option*, as it pertains to the standard lease-option strategy being taught today, is a misnomer. What is being taught today is really a sublease-option strategy, which requires investors to lease a property and then sublease it to a so-called tenant-buyer. Thus, the correct term for this strategy is *sublease-options* and not lease-options. This is exactly why in the first part of this chapter I give you the lowdown on the standard lease-option strategy that is being taught today. And once I have finished telling you all of the details on the potential risks and problems that lease-options pose, I show you how to properly structure a lease and option transaction so that you can use the low-risk, low-cost lease and option strategy to profit from single-family houses.

Why the Risk versus Reward Ratio for Sublease-Options Is Way Out of Whack

First off, the risk versus reward ratio for sublease-options is way out of whack! In other words, the risk potential that is associated with using sublease-options far outweighs the profit potential! There are just too many things that can go wrong with a sublease-option deal, which a lessee has absolutely no control over. For example, during the sublease-option period, any of the following can and usually do occur:

1. The tenant-buyer fails to make lease payments and must be evicted.
2. The tenant-buyer cannot be evicted from the property because a court rules that he or she has an equitable interest in the property and must be foreclosed on instead of evicted.
3. The tenant-buyer commits a wanton act of malicious vandalism and destroys the leased property.
4. The owner refuses to sell the property after the tenant-buyer has exercised his or her option.
5. The owner refuses to sell the property at the agreed-upon purchase price after the tenant-buyer has exercised his or her option.
6. The property under lease-option is damaged or destroyed by fire, storm, or earthquake, and the tenant-buyer must be relocated.

The Sublease-Option Strategy Requires the Lessee to Become a Landlord

The standard sublease-option strategy being pushed today involves leasing a property and then subleasing it to a tenant-buyer. This requires the lessee (tenant) to become a lessor (landlord) responsible for managing the tenant-buyer. A sublease is also known as a *sandwich lease*, which is generally defined as: "A lease agreement in which the lessee (tenant) becomes a lessor (landlord) by subleasing the property under lease to a sublessee (tenant) who takes possession of the property." Under a typical sublease-option arrangement, an investor signs a lease-option agreement with a property owner and then subleases the property to a third party, known as a tenant-buyer, by using a sublease-option agreement. It is sort of the real estate equivalent of a threesome, in which the following three parties are involved in two separate lease-option transactions:

1. *Lessor-optionor:* The owner of the property being lease-optioned.
2. *Lessee-optionee:* The party leasing the property from the owner with an option to buy.
3. *Tenant-buyer:* The party subleasing the property from the lessee-optionee with an option to buy.

The problem with this scenario is that 99 percent of all investors who get involved in a sublease-option transaction do not know diddly squat about being a residential landlord. As a result, whenever they have any type of problem with a tenant-buyer, they are clueless about the correct way to solve it. For example, I recently received an e-mail from a lessee-optionee in Atlanta, Georgia, who wanted to know how to go about evicting a tenant-buyer in Georgia. I told her to log on to the state of Georgia web site and look up the residential tenant and landlord act online. The point that I am making here is that this person had never even bothered to take the time to acquire the most basic knowledge about being a residential landlord in Georgia, even though residential rental housing is one of the most highly regulated businesses in America. In most cases, this ignorance of basic property management fundamentals turns out to be a recipe for financial disaster.

Why the Sublease-Option Strategy Isn't Financially Feasible

The main reason I am not a fan of the sublease-option strategy that is being taught today is that it is not financially feasible. In other words, there is just not enough profit in most sublease-option transactions to make them financially worthwhile. For example, under a typical sublease-option scenario, a lessee-optionee would be lucky to receive from a tenant-buyer a $1,000 option fee and a monthly sublease payment that is $100 above his or her lease payment. In most cases, what appears on paper as a $100 a month positive cash flow really is not. This is because most investors involved in sublease-option transactions never bother to factor in the amount of time they spend managing property as a business expense. If they did, they would come to the quick realization that they are working for minimum wage. I do not know about you, but to me, the prospect of working for minimum wage, especially as a self-employed real estate investor, has zero appeal! However, low wages are not the only thing that most sublease-option investors have to look forward to. There is also the very distinct possibility of having to evict a tenant-buyer and pay the lease payments while the property is vacant, along with the costs associated with finding another tenant-buyer. And these out-of-pocket lease payments and other costs that can never be recouped under a typical sublease-option scenario are the reason sublease-options usually do not make any financial sense. I know a former sublease-option investor in Richmond, Virginia, who ended up paying over $4,700 in property repairs after he refused to give his tenant-buyer a six-month extension, and the enraged tenant totally trashed the place before skipping town. All in all, this investor claims to have lost $6,300 on his first and last sublease-option deal.

Most Investors Don't Have the Cash
Reserves to Subsidize Sublease-Options

The fact of the matter is that most real estate investors are woefully undercapitalized and do not have the deep pockets or cash reserves that are usually needed to subsidize sublease-option deals. Few serial sublease-option investors are around because most people go broke supporting their first sublease-option deal! This lack of operating capital creates a domino effect whenever there is any type of financial emergency. For example, when a tenant-buyer fails to pay the monthly sublease payment, the lessee usually has no money to make the lease payment to the property owner, which forces the owner to initiate eviction proceedings against the lessee for nonpayment of rent. This in turn forces the lessee to start the eviction process against the tenant-buyer for failing to pay the rent. And if the lessee cannot come up with the money to pay the lease payment, the lessee will end up losing the real estate option, and the only thing he or she will have to show for their time, effort, and money will be an eviction on his or her record.

Sublease-Options Appeal Mostly to
Credit-Challenged Would-Be Homebuyers

Another very good reason I am not a proponent of the sublease-option strategy is that, for the most part, the only people that sublease-options appeal to are credit-challenged, would-be homebuyers with a track record of being financially irresponsible. These are people who lack the income and creditworthiness required to obtain a mortgage or deed of trust loan in order to finance the purchase of a home. They are also the same type of people who require constant prodding in order to get them to take care of the property and pay their rent on time. The real problem with this class of tenant-buyers is that 9 out of 10 of them will never be able to exercise their option and actually buy the property. What generally happens in cases like this is that the real estate option expires because the tenant-buyer was not able to obtain financing in order to buy the property. And the sublease-option investor ends up with nothing to show for all of the time, effort, aggravation, and money spent on the deal.

The Standard Lease-Option Agreement Violates the Due-on-Sale Clause in Loans

Although I know of no case nationwide where a residential mortgage or deed of trust lender has declared a loan to be in default because the borrower signed a lease-option agreement on the property securing the mortgage or deed of trust and promissory note, you need to know that the lender's discovery of a lease-option agreement can trigger the due-on-sale clause contained in residential mortgage and deed of trust loans. Section 591.2 (b) of Title 12, Banks and Banking, of the Code of Federal Regulations states:

> Due-on-sale clause means a contract provision which authorizes the lender, at its option, to declare immediately due and payable sums secured by the lender's security instrument upon a sale or transfer of all or any part of the real property securing the loan without the lender's prior written consent. For purposes of this definition, a sale or transfer means the conveyance of real property of any right, title or interest therein, whether legal or equitable, whether voluntary or involuntary, by outright sale, deed, installment sale contract, land contract, contract for deed, leasehold interest with a term greater than three years, lease-option contract or any other method of conveyance of real property interests.

Many Equity-Skimming Scams Involve the Use of Lease-Options

You also need to know that many equity-skimming scams involve the use of lease-options. Equity skimming occurs when a property owner uses any part of the rent, assets, proceeds, income, or other funds derived from the property covered by a mortgage or deed of trust loan as personal funds. In a typical lease-option equity-skimming scam, a property owner collects an option fee and security deposit upfront and then collects lease payments for months on end without ever making a single loan payment to the lender. This goes on until the lender finally forecloses on the loan and evicts the unsuspecting lessee or tenant-buyer. Under Chapter 12, United States Code, Section 1709-2, a person who engages in equity skimming is defined as:

> Whoever, with intent to defraud, willfully engages in a pattern or practice of:
>
> (1) purchasing one- to four-family dwellings (including condominiums and cooperatives) which are subject to a loan in default at time of purchase or in default within one year subsequent to the purchase and the loan is secured by a mortgage or deed of trust insured or held by the Secretary of Housing and Urban Development or guaranteed by the Department of Veterans Affairs, or the loan is made by the Department of Veterans Affairs,
>
> (2) failing to make payments under the mortgage or deed of trust as the payments become due, regardless of whether the purchaser is obligated on the loan, and
>
> (3) applying or authorizing the application of rents from such dwellings for his own use, shall be fined not more than $250,000 or imprisoned not more than 5 years, or both. This section shall apply to a purchaser of such a dwelling, or a beneficial owner under any business organization or trust purchasing such dwelling, or to an officer, director, or agent of any such purchaser. Nothing in this section shall apply to the purchaser of only one such dwelling.

Most Lease-Option Transactions Are Really Installment Sales

Finally, the standard lease-option that everyone seems to have gone gaga over is a lease-option in name only. In the real world, this is called an *installment sale*. Why? Because under the terms contained in a standard lease-option agreement, the relationship between the parties is that of debtor and creditor, and not that of lessee-optionee and lessor-optionor. This debtor-creditor relationship is created whenever the terms of a lease-option call for the property owner (lessor-optionor) to credit the option consideration and a fixed portion of the monthly lease payment toward the purchase price when the real estate option is exercised. Once this debtor-creditor relationship is created, the tenant (lessee-optionee) has an equitable or ownership interest instead of a leasehold interest in the property being lease-optioned. When a lease-option agreement gives the lessee-optionee an equitable interest in the property being lease-optioned, it becomes an installment sales agreement and not a lease-option agreement. This means that if the tenant must be evicted, the owner could be forced to file a costly and time-consuming lawsuit to foreclose instead of an eviction lawsuit. Please consider this when you contemplate ignoring my advice and becoming a party to a standard sublease-option transaction!

A Low-Cost, Low-Risk Lease and Option Strategy That Makes Financial Sense

I hope that you heed my advice and avoid using the high-risk sublease-option strategy, which I have written about here. Instead, use a low-risk lease and option strategy, which involves buying a low-cost real estate option on an undervalued single-family house that you can lease at a below-market rental rate. This way, you not only save money on housing costs but also have the opportunity to profit from the property's appreciation in value. The lease and option strategy provides a relatively low-cost, low-risk way to gain control of an undervalued single-family house, without having to incur the cost and financial liability that goes along with outright ownership. And best of all, when you use the lease and option strategy that I am writing about here, you do not have to become a landlord and babysit tenant-buyers. All you have to do is move in and market the house to potential buyers. In the meantime, you get all of the benefits of homeownership—less the tax benefits—without ever having to:

1. Qualify for a loan.
2. Pay a down payment.
3. Pay closing costs.
4. Pay for repairs.
5. Buy any property.

The Lease and Option Strategy Involves Two Separate Transactions

The lease and option strategy that I am writing about here involves two separate transactions: a straight real estate option transaction exactly like the type that has been covered extensively in this book and a genuine lease transaction in which the:

1. Relationship between the parties is that of lessee (tenant) and lessor (landlord).
2. Lessee has a leasehold interest in the property being leased.

3. Lessee agrees to pay a monthly lease payment.
4. Lessor agrees to maintain the property during the lease period.

Why You Must Always Use Separate Lease and Real Estate Option Agreements

If you do not get anything else from this chapter, please get this: Always use separate lease and real estate option agreements to document your lease and option transactions. And never, ever use a standard lease-option agreement, which includes both the lease and the option to purchase in the same agreement. That is a big no-no. Why is that? Because under the terms contained in a standard boilerplate lease-option agreement, once the lessee-optionee defaults on the lease and is evicted, the option agreement becomes null and void, too. However, when you use separate lease and option agreements, the option agreement will not automatically get wiped out if you default on the terms of the lease agreement and are evicted. The separate option agreement will still be valid until it is exercised or expires. And you will still have an opportunity to profit from the house under option. Also, in order to use the lease and option strategy that I am telling you about in this chapter, both your lease and real estate option agreements must include assignment clauses that allow you to sell your agreements to a third party without the property owner's permission.

Record Separate Memorandums of Option and Lease in the Public Records

I highly recommend that you do not let the cat out of the bag by recording a copy of your real estate option agreement in the official public records. In my opinion, recording the entire agreement only blabs the sale price and terms to the whole world, which could come back to bite you in the backside later on. Instead, I recommend that you record a separate memorandum of real estate option agreement, like the sample in Chapter 17, and a memorandum of lease agreement, like the sample on page 49.

How a Lease and Option Transaction Works

Here is a step-by-step outline of the mechanics of a lease and option transaction:

Step 1: The lessee (tenant) agrees to lease a property from the owner (lessor).

Step 2: The lessee buys a real estate option from the lessor to purchase the property under lease.

FORM 5.1   Sample Memorandum of Lease Agreement

This memorandum of lease agreement made this ninth day of July 2005, is for the purpose of recording and giving notice of a lease agreement made between David D. Jones, known hereinafter as the Lessor, and Donald S. Reed, known hereinafter as the Lessee, in which Lessor agrees to lease to Lessee that certain real property known as 45735 Hillsborough Avenue, Tampa, Florida 33603, and legally described as: Lots 47, 48 and 49 of Carter's subdivision according to map or plat thereof as recorded in plat book 69, page 89, of the public records of Hillsborough County, Florida, which was executed between the Lessor and Lessee on the ninth day of July 2005 and which will expire at twelve o'clock midnight on the eighth day of July 2006.

IN WITNESS WHEREOF, Lessor and Lessee have set their hands the date aforesaid

David D. Jones   Donald S. Reed

Lessor   Lessee

Step 3: The real estate option grants the lessee-optionee the exclusive, unrestricted, and irrevocable right and option to purchase the property under lease at a fixed purchase price during the option period.

Step 4: The lessee-optionee can assign or exercise the real estate option or let it expire.

Step 5: Once exercised, the real estate option agreement turns into a bilateral purchase agreement, in which the lessee-optionee becomes buyer and lessor-optionor, the seller.

Step 6: The seller transfers the property's title to the buyer when the transaction is closed.

Six Key Terms That Must Be Negotiated in All Lease and Option Agreements

In addition to following the negotiating advice that I outline in Chapter 13, you must obtain the following six key terms when negotiating lease and option agreements:

1. Two-year lease agreement.
2. Two-year real estate option agreement.
3. Fixed purchase price that is at least 20 percent below the property's current market value.
4. Rental rate that is at least 10 percent below the property's fair market rental rate.
5. One-year extension clause in the lease agreement.
6. One-year extension clause in the real estate option agreement.

Insure Your Personal Property with a Renters' Insurance Policy

When you are a tenant leasing property, I highly recommend that you insure your personal property with a renters' insurance policy. Most renter's insurance policies provide coverage against fire and theft to personal property and personal liability coverage for injuries and damages caused by tenant neglect. Log on to the following web sites to find adequate renters' insurance coverage:

Geico Renters' Insurance: www.homeowners.geico.com/renters.html

InsWeb: www.insweb.com

Quote Fetcher: www.quotefetcher.com/renters-insurance.htm

NETQUOTE: www.netquote.com

Require All Lease Payments Be Made to a Licensed Loan-Servicing Company

As a lessee-optionee, the only way to avoid being a victim in an equity-skimming scam is to require that all lease payments be made directly to a licensed loan-servicing company. For example, the loan-servicing company would take the money they receive from you as lease payments and use it to make loan payments directly to the lender. This way, you have verifiable proof that the loan payment is being made, and you are not funding the property owner's equity-skimming scam. The following web sites are for two licensed loan-servicing companies that provide service nationwide:

North American Loan Servicing: www.sellerloans.com/index.htm

PLM Lender Services, Inc.: www.plmweb.com/index.html

The Best Type of House to Use the Lease and Option Strategy On

The best type of house to use the lease and option strategy on is a three-bedroom, two-bathroom house with an attached garage and fenced-in backyard in a stable, middle-income neighborhood, which is conveniently located near:

1. Medical facilities.
2. Shopping malls.
3. Schools, parks, and playgrounds.
4. Military bases.
5. Office and industrial parks.

The Property Owners Who Are Most Likely to Agree to a Lease and Option Deal

The types of property owners who are most likely to agree to lease their house with an option to buy are usually:

1. Owners of vacant houses.
2. Owners being relocated out of town by their employer on short notice.
3. Military personnel being transferred on short notice.
4. Absentee owners who reside out of town.

Lease and Option Properties Are Relatively Easy to Market to Potential Buyers

The best part about using the lease and option strategy is that it is relatively easy to market a single-family house that is under lease and option when you are the tenant residing in the property. The fact is, you do not even have to place a for-sale sign on the property. All you have to do is place a well-written ad in your local newspaper that directs interested parties to a telephone number or a web site address. This way, you avoid being pestered by nosy neighbors and people who are just out looking, but not serious buyers. Chapter 19 has complete step-by-step instructions on how to package, market, and sell your real estate options for maximum profit.

CHAPTER 6

How You Can Use Options to Profit from Properties with Correctable Problems

The one thing that the most profitable types of option properties all have in common is that none of them will ever be mistaken for a so-called blue chip property. The term *blue chip* is used to describe properties that have a flawless appearance, are in pristine condition, and are situated in prime locations. As you will soon see, none of the properties that I write about in this chapter fit that bill. In fact, the chances that the average real estate option investor has of ever putting a trophy-type property under option are slim and none. I say this because the owners of highly sought-after properties can pretty much name their own sale price and terms and have no compelling reason to sell an option to anyone whereas owners of vacant properties with various types of problems, which scare off most prospective buyers, are in no position to be choosy when it comes to how they sell their property. And this is exactly why one of the most profitable types of properties to buy real estate options on is properties with correctable problems such as:

1. Title problems that cloud a property's title and prevent the owner from having a clear and marketable title.

2. Maintenance problems that result when routine building maintenance is deferred over a long period of time and causes the property to be in a run-down condition.

3. Structural problems resulting from damage done by sinkholes and earthquakes, which cause building foundations to crack and sink.

4. Code violation problems that occur when owners neglect the upkeep of their properties, which causes them to be cited for building, fire safety, and health code violations.

5. Stigma problems that affect properties that are located near various nuisances, such as sewage treatments plants, hazardous waste material, halfway houses for criminals, and group homes for sex offenders.

6. Property damage problems caused by man-made disasters such as wildfires and natural disasters like hurricanes, tornadoes, floods, and earthquakes.

The key to being successful with this option strategy is to put only properties with problems that can be corrected under option. And to do this, you must know the difference between correctable and noncorrectable property problems. For example, almost all property title problems can be corrected by a knowledgeable real estate attorney or land title professional. However, a building with a major flaw that affects its structural integrity and cannot be repaired, is not the type of problem property that you want to buy an option on.

How You Should Use the Problem Property Option Strategy

The biggest mistake that investors sometimes make when using this strategy is that they bite off more than they can chew. They do this by trying to correct the problem affecting the property themselves, instead of reselling their option to a niche investor who specializes in turning problem properties around. You should be using this strategy the same way that I told you to use the obsolescent property strategy in Chapter 4. And your objective after you put a problem property under option should always be to find a buyer for the property. The only exception to this is properties with title problems that can be quickly and inexpensively corrected in order to put the property's title in a marketable condition and greatly increase its resale value. In cases like this, you would correct the title problem and then resell your option to a third party or exercise the option yourself and buy the property. I realize that some of you reading this may wonder why problem property owners do not correct the problems themselves and then sell the property by owner or list the property for sale through a real estate broker. The truth of the matter is that most owners do not have the money, knowledge, time, or desire to solve their own problem property woes. Plus, most real estate brokers are very reluctant to list any type of problem property out of fear that the buyer will come back and sue them after the sale, and they will somehow be found liable for wrongdoing. And those owners who do attempt to sell their problem properties themselves usually do a pretty lousy job of marketing and end up with no takers. They do not know how to conduct market research to identify prospective buyers who could possibly have a use for their property. And luckily for us savvy option investors, they usually fail to look beyond the borders of their own local real estate market for so-called niche investors, who specialize in buying properties with every imaginable type of problem. These niche problem property investors run property wanted ads in professional real estate trade publications and newspapers with national circulations, such as the *Wall Street Journal* and the *New York Times*. For example, I have resold options on two problem properties that were contaminated with hazardous waste material to niche investors who specialize in cleaning up contaminated properties, whom I found through ads in trade publications.

Government Agencies Can Be an Excellent Source of Problem Property Leads

One of the best sources of problem property leads that is often overlooked by most investors is local, county, and state government agencies. For example, one of the types of properties that I buy options on is vacant commercial properties that have been repeatedly cited for non-structural code violations. I have chosen this particular type of property because these properties are in steady supply and are relatively easy to find in Hillsborough County, Florida. The code enforcement departments for both the city of Tampa and Hillsborough County maintain files on all of the properties that have been cited for code violations. Plus, these properties have bright fluorescent orange condemnation notices conspicuously posted on them. The following local, county, and state government agencies are all sources of problem property leads:

1. Local police and sheriffs' departments have reports available on arrests that involved real property used in crimes that has been damaged. Many times, these are residential rental properties that have been used to manufacture illegal drugs and are owned by landlords who do not have the money or desire to make them fit for human habitation.

2. Local and county fire departments have reports available on properties that have been cited for fire code violations and properties that have been totally destroyed by fire and water damage. In some cases, these burnt-out properties are uninsured, and the owners do not have the money to rebuild. Or, the owners are insured, but they lack the desire to rebuild.

3. Local and county code enforcement departments maintain records on properties that have been cited for building and safety code violations or ordered condemned for demolition. In many instances, these properties belong to owners who do not have the time, money, or desire to make the repairs needed to bring their property into compliance with the code.

4. Local and county public health departments keep records on commercial and residential properties that have been cited for health code violations. In some instances, the health violations are severe enough for the health department to declare the property unfit for human habitation and order it vacated.

Three Types of Problem Properties That Scare Off Most Conventional Investors

The three types of problem properties that scare off most conventional real estate investors are:

1. *Stigmatized properties:* These are properties that have a stigma attached to them because of some traumatic event that has occurred on the property, or the property is located near undesirable properties and nuisances.

2. *Contaminated properties:* These are properties that are contaminated by chemicals, mold, nauseating odors, or accumulations of toxic bird droppings, or they are infested with rodents, insects, or birds.

3. *Condemned properties:* These are properties that have been condemned by government agencies for building, health, safety, or fire code violations.

Why Properties with Problems Don't Scare Me

Personally, I like properties with problems that scare off most conventional real estate investors. Generally, these are properties with correctable problems that appear to be complicated and usually require some sort of specialized knowledge in order to be solved. However, in most cases, it is the common misperception of how difficult the problem is to solve than the actual problem itself that scares off most conventional real estate investors. For example, I specialize in buying real estate options on small, vacant, condemned commercial properties that are structurally sound but in dire need of an industrial-strength cleaning. Most conventional investors are instantly turned off by this type of property simply because of outward appearance, which generally looks far worse than its actual physical condition. They cannot see beyond the filth and grime that can be easily washed off with a pressure washer and the smelly garbage and accumulation of junk that can be inexpensively hauled away. However, what scares most conventional investors more than the sight and smell of a condemned property is the very thought of having to deal with the local governmental bureaucracy in order to bring the property into compliance with the building code so that a certificate of occupancy can be issued to the owner. The fact is I have never had a problem with any government agency regarding the turnaround of a condemned property because, before I ever buy an option on a condemned property, I first meet with the local code enforcement inspection supervisor who is responsible for the area where the property is located. I do this to go over the code violation inspection citations to find out the bare minimum that needs to be done in order to bring the property into compliance. This way, I know exactly what needs to be done and have a ballpark idea of the cost to do it. And once I put a condemned property under option, I get it into compliance within 30 days or less. I get along well with code enforcement officials because I always act in a professional manner and make their jobs easy by not giving them a hard time.

How to Buy Options on Properties with Clouded Titles

The term *cloud,* as it relates to real property, is a claim or encumbrance recorded against a property's title that prevents the owner from having a *clear and marketable title* to the property. And the problem with a clouded title is that title insurance companies will almost never issue a title insurance policy that insures against a cloud on a property's title. Instead, they will issue a title policy that lists the cloud as an exception to the policy, which means that the so-called exception clouding the title is not covered by the policy. The most common problems that cloud a property's title are:

1. Mortgage and deed of trust loans that have been discharged or paid off, but the lender never recorded a satisfaction of lien in the public records.
2. Missing heirs that must be located to sign the deed and transfer the title to the property.
3. Judgment liens recorded against the property's title and the lienholders cannot be located.

4. Multiple parties claiming ownership of a property by recording quit claim deeds.

5. Unsettled property boundary disputes involving flawed surveys.

When you buy an option on a property with title problems, there are two very important things that you must do. First, you must buy an 8- to 12-month option so that you have ample time to complete a quiet title action in court. Second, you must obtain the property owner's written authorization to allow you to file a lawsuit to quiet title on the owner's behalf. I always have the owner give me a limited power of attorney that allows me to take whatever actions are necessary to quiet the title.

How to Have a Cloud
Removed from a Property's Title

In most cases, the only way to remove a cloud on a property title is to go through a legal process known as a quiet title action or lawsuit, during which an adverse claim or cloud on the title to real property is removed. In the lawsuit, the owner or plaintiff names all of the defendants who might have an interest in the property's title, to include prior owners, descendants, and lienholders. However, in some cases, a quiet title action is a so-called friendly lawsuit, in which there is no opposition from defendants. In those cases, a lawsuit is filed primarily to give the public constructive notice of the plaintiff's claim. The time frame to complete a quiet title action usually depends on the actions taken by the plaintiffs, the amount of time the plaintiffs have to respond to the complaint that was filed with the lawsuit, and any statutory public notice requirements that must be met. For example, here in Florida, it can take anywhere from three to six months to complete a quiet title action. After all of the statutory procedures involved in a quiet title action have been completed, the judge hearing the case will make a decision based on the evidence presented by both parties. And if the lawsuit is decided in the plaintiff's favor, the judge will order that a final judgment be issued that removes the cloud from the property's title.

Once I have property with title problems under option, I hire an experienced professional title abstractor or researcher to do a title search at the public records library in the county where the property's title is recorded. And just as soon as I get the property's title report, I send it to my real estate attorney, who files a quiet title lawsuit, in which all the parties claiming an interest in the property are named as defendants. At the same time, the required legal notices are published in the court's paper of record to give the public notice of the lawsuit. I usually end up paying my attorney between $800 and $1,200 to handle a quiet title action for me.

How to Buy Options on Properties Destroyed by Natural and Man-Made Disasters

First things first: You must be very careful when using this option strategy, so that you are not perceived as just another sleazy opportunist trying to take advantage of the plight of disaster victims. And this is why it is best that you never contact any property owners in disaster areas until after the dust has had a chance to settle. I am telling you this because after every man-made and natural disaster, there is always a segment of the population, especially in the areas that have been the hardest hit, who throw in the towel and take their insurance money and run. And property owners who have been reimbursed by their insurer for their loss but, for whatever reason, have no desire to rebuild are the owners who are most likely to sell an option to purchase their destroyed property. Savvy option investors can buy a one- to two-year option to purchase the property at a bargain price, clear away the rubble, and wait until the recovery is well underway, and then resell or exercise their option. Building lots with existing utility hookups appeal to homebuilders because they are ready to build on and they avoid paying impact fees to local and state government agencies. This strategy has a lot of profit potential because of the lack of competition from other investors. I recommend that you use the following methods to locate property owners in disaster areas who would be willing to sell investors an option to buy their destroyed property:

1. Contact owners by handing out flyers because mail service may be interrupted for quite a while.
2. Place ads on billboards as the rates should be cheaper due to local economic conditions.
3. Buy radio and TV spot advertising.
4. Place classified ads in local newspapers.

CHAPTER 7

How to Use Options to Control Properties That Can Be Rezoned for More Profitable Uses

An often overlooked, but very profitable, option strategy involves buying options on properties that can be rezoned for more profitable uses. Rezoning is required whenever a property owner wants to use his or her property for a purpose that does not conform to its current zoning classification. The rezoning strategy outlined in this chapter involves buying an 8- to 12-month option for the purpose of controlling a piece of property while awaiting approval to have the property's zoning classification changed to a more profitable use. And once the rezoning request is approved, you can either resell your option or exercise it and buy the property yourself. Rezoning can be very profitable, as converting a property to another use by changing its land use or zoning classification is usually much less expensive than acquiring land and putting up a new building from scratch. Your best bet when using this rezoning strategy is to find a vacant property in an area that is changing from residential to commercial use and where recent rezoning requests have been approved. I refer to these as *emerging commercial areas,* and the main reason you want to buy options in this type of area is that you are less likely to meet any organized opposition to your rezoning application. As you will learn later in this chapter, organized opposition from anti-rezoning zealots is generally the biggest obstacle that investors face when going through the rezoning approval process. However, I am forewarning you that, in many instances, investors can be their own worst enemy during the rezoning approval process, especially when they fail to grasp the exact mechanics of rezoning procedures in their area and try to cut corners by not going through all of the required steps. The very last thing that you want to do during the rezoning approval process is get on the wrong side of the bureaucrats who make up the staffs of local government planning and zoning agencies by attempting to go around them and bypass their approval of your application. I say this because once you have been identified as someone who does not want to play by the rules, these so-called public servants will make you toe the line and do everything exactly by the book and will cut you absolutely no slack. Plus, the staff members will more than likely recommend to the locally elected officials who have the final say on rezoning applications that your application be denied. And 9 out of 10 times, such a recommendation is enough to get the politicians to say no to your application. My bottom line advice for investors going through the rezoning approval process is to do your homework, leave your ego at home, and adopt an attitude of cooperation.

Beginning investors often ask me why property owners would sell an option on a piece of property that can be rezoned to a more profitable use. They do this because they do not understand that average property owners do not have an entrepreneurial bone in their body. And the idea of rezoning their property probably never even crossed their mind. But even if they did think of it, most property owners do not have the knowledge, money, or desire to apply for rezoning approval themselves. Or, if they did want their property rezoned, most owners are usually intimidated by the rezoning application and approval process, petrified of speaking in public, and worried about what their family and friends will think when their appearance before the zoning commission is broadcast on the local public access television channel.

The Definition of Rezoning

Land use and zoning professionals generally define the term *rezoning* as: "The act of changing the zoning or land use classification of a parcel of land to permit the property to be used for another purpose."

How the Rezoning Process Works in Most Jurisdictions

In most jurisdictions, rezoning is a quasi-legal process that requires the approval of locally elected officials, such as town council members, city council members, aldermen, and county commissioners or supervisors. And this is why often rezoning requests can become highly politicized. Most planning and zoning committees, commissions, and boards are composed of a chairperson, who is an elected official, and members, who are local citizens appointed by elected officials. A property owner or petitioner submits a rezoning application to the planning or zoning agency, who reviews the application and passes their recommendations along to the elected officials, who have the final say in the matter. The elected officials then hold public hearings during which all interested parties can be heard before a final vote on the rezoning request is taken. But getting a rezoning request approved is often not easy, and it can end up being a long and arduous process. The rezoning application review process is usually very cumbersome and often requires input from numerous local government agencies. In some jurisdictions, it can take up to four months between the time a rezoning application is filed and when it is placed on the planning or zoning agency's agenda to be heard at from one to three public meetings. To learn all of the details of how the zoning process works in your area, log on to the local government's web site and look under planning, zoning, or land use. To see the actual rezoning approval process in action, attend a public rezoning hearing in person or, if available, watch one on local public access cable television. In most areas, the rezoning process is composed of the following steps:

Step 1: Meet with planning or zoning agency staff members to have your application reviewed.

Step 2: Submit a completed rezoning application that includes an affidavit to authorize the agent form bearing the notarized signature of the property owner, and pay the applicable rezoning application fee.

Step 3: Send written notification of the rezoning request to all the surrounding property owners.

Step 4: Make a rezoning presentation before the local planning or zoning hearing master.

Step 5: The planning or zoning hearing master makes a recommendation on the rezoning request to the local governing body where the property is located.

Step 6: Attend one or more public hearings in front of elected officials and planning or zoning agency staff members, during which public comments are heard and staff members make recommendations to elected officials.

Step 7: Attend a final public hearing in front of elected officials before they take a final vote to approve or deny your rezoning application.

For further information on planning, land use, and zoning, log on to the following web site: www. plannersweb.com.

What You Must Include in Your Rezoning Application Package

In most jurisdictions, a rezoning application package must include the following items:

1. Completed and signed rezoning application.
2. Street address of property.
3. Legal description for property.
4. List of surrounding property owners located within a specific radius of the property.
5. Written statement explaining why the change of the property's land use classification is being requested.
6. Description of the proposed use of the property.
7. A site plan of the property drawn to scale.
8. A location map showing where the property is located within the city or county.
9. A copy of the property's survey.
10. Aerial photographs of the property.

When I am putting a rezoning application package together, I do all of the research and legwork and file all of the necessary paperwork with the appropriate government agency. But when it comes time to attend a rezoning hearing before a so-called zoning master, I sit on the sidelines and hire an experienced attorney whose specialty is land use and zoning. I do this because my attorney is an expert at cutting through all of the bureaucratic gobbledygook and getting rezoning requests approved on the first go around. This way, I do not have to waste my time worrying about getting involved in a long, drawn-out battle with government bureaucrats and grandstanding politicians.

Why You Must Know Who the Anti-Rezoning Zealots Are in Your Area

In addition to knowing the mechanics of the rezoning process in your area, you must also know who the anti-rezoning zealots are in your area. In virtually every hamlet, village, town, city, and county across America, there is at least one anti-rezoning zealot, who automatically opposes all rezoning changes out of hand.

And the rezoning approval process can become very political when civic, neighborhood, and homeowners' associations become involved. For example, in South Tampa, there is a very vocal woman who fancies herself as an elderly matron and makes it a habit to oppose all rezoning changes in her neighborhood and all surrounding neighborhoods. Any time anyone submits a rezoning request for a property located within these neighborhoods, she and her cronies complain to politicians, whine to the local media, protest at public zoning hearings, and are a real menace to real estate investors. Needless to say, I have not filed any rezoning applications for properties located in her neck of the woods.

Best to Take the Path of Least Resistance When Applying for Rezoning Approval

When it comes to selecting properties for rezoning, I am a firm believer in taking the path of least resistance. This is why I buy options only on properties that can be relatively easy to rezone to more profitable uses, that is, properties that are well below the public radar screen and not located close to well-established neighborhoods inhabited by vocal activists who make it a habit to protest all rezoning requests at public rezoning hearings. In other words, you will not find me buying an option on a single-family house in a tranquil residential neighborhood with the expectation of getting a rezoning request for an adult business approved. As a general rule of thumb, when I am looking for a property that can be rezoned to a more profitable use, I look for properties that are located in emerging commercial areas, where rezoning requests have been relatively easy to get approved. I specialize in single-family houses on double-sized lots that can be rezoned and easily converted into professional office space for doctors, attorneys, accountants, and dentists. I want double-sized lots to make certain that there is ample room for parking spaces and landscape buffers at the property lines.

How to Quickly Determine if a Potential Option Property Can Be Rezoned

Before I ever approach an owner about buying an option on a property that would increase in value if it could be rezoned to a more profitable use, I first research the property to determine if it can be rezoned. The quickest way that I know to determine if a potential option property can be rezoned to a more profitable use is to contact both your local planning and zoning agencies. For example, where I live, both the city of Tampa and the county of Hillsborough have zoning counselors whose job is to guide residents through the rezoning process. I use the services of these public servants to help me research the property under consideration for purchase and advise me on the probability of my rezoning request being approved. The county also holds pre-submission conferences, where rezoning applicants can meet with staff representatives to go over their proposed zoning change. I then decide whether to pursue the property based on my research and the amount of resistance that a rezoning request would likely draw. I suggest that you do as I do and follow these nine steps to determine if a property can be rezoned to a more profitable use:

Step 1: Verify the zoning designation of the property.

Step 2: Review previous rezoning applications for the property.

Step 3: Review government moratoriums affecting the property.

Step 4: Review comprehensive land use studies that include the property.

Step 5: Verify the zoning designations of the surrounding properties.

Step 6: Review the rezoning application files for the surrounding properties.

Step 7: Review special zoning exceptions and variances for the surrounding properties.

Step 8: Review the rezoning application files of similar rezoning requests.

Step 9: Solicit comments about rezoning the property from the planning and zoning agency staffs.

What You Need to Do When Buying an Option on a Property You Want Rezoned

When you buy an option on a property with the intention of applying to have it rezoned for a more profitable use, you must be certain to obtain the optionor's written approval, allowing you to represent him or her before the government agencies that regulate the rezoning process in your city or county.

In my area, this document is called an *affidavit to authorize agent,* and it gives the property owner's authorized agent the right to sign any documents necessary to file a rezoning application. Make certain that you have this crucial document signed by the optionor and acknowledged at the same time the option agreement and title transfer documents are signed and acknowledged. You must also know the approximate time between when a rezoning application is submitted and when it is approved and put on the books. In some jurisdictions, it can take from three to six months, depending on how frequent the approving authority meets and their workload, to get a rezoning application approved. And this is exactly why it is imperative that you negotiate an 8- to 12-month option period when using the rezoning strategy, so that you are covered in case the application and approval process takes longer than normal. I learned this lesson the hard way on my first rezoning deal when I was given some bad advice by an incompetent attorney and signed a three-month option deal. Right after I signed the option agreement, I got a rude awakening when I learned that the county had a three-month backlog of zoning applications, which my legal whiz had failed to tell me about. I fired the clueless attorney on the spot and paid the optionor $2,500 to extend the option period for another five months. And seven months later, I finally got the property's zoning classification changed from residential to professional office and had a $20,000 payday when I resold my option to an attorney.

CHAPTER 8

How You Can Use the LASH Strategy to Profit from Long-Term, Flat-Rate Master Leases and Real Estate Options

In Chapter 5, I told you how to use the lease and option strategy to profit from single-family houses. Now, I tell you how to use the LASH strategy to profit from long-term, flat-rate master leases and real estate options. LASH is an acronym that I have coined for "lease and sublease higher." The LASH strategy involves making money through the use of master leases, subleases, or sandwich leases and real estate options. The LASH strategy was used on the Empire State Building in New York City from 1961 to 2002. During this time, the National Historic Landmark was operated under a master lease. The World Trade Center was operated under a 99-year master lease before it was destroyed in the infamous terrorist attack of September 11, 2001. However, before you go adding LASH to your repertoire of real estate option strategies, you first need to know:

1. How the LASH strategy works.
2. Where to find valid lease agreements.
3. Why you must always use separate master lease and real estate option agreements.
4. The key provisions that must be included in your master lease agreements.
5. The key provisions that must be included in your sublease agreements.
6. How to best protect your position as lessee.
7. The key points to negotiate in your master lease.

8. The best types of properties to use the LASH strategy on.

9. How to thoroughly screen tenant applicants.

How the LASH Strategy Works

In a LASH transaction, there are three parties:

1. The property owner, who is the landlord or lessor.

2. The tenant, who is the lessee and the sublessor.

3. The sublease tenant, who is the sublessee.

There is really nothing very complicated about how the LASH strategy works. It is nothing more than the old BLASH—buy low and sell higher—strategy applied to leasing. For example, when using the LASH strategy, a tenant or lessee signs a long-term (three- to five-year) flat-rate master lease with a landlord or lessor. The master lease agreement creates a leasehold estate, giving the tenant the right to possess, use, and sublease the property. Once the tenant subleases the property to a sublease tenant or sublessee, the tenant becomes a sublessor. In a LASH transaction, the tenant acts as a middleman, leasing the property directly from the owner and then subleasing it to a sublease tenant. To illustrate, let us suppose that a tenant has a $2,500 a month master lease on a small commercial property, which is subleased for $3,300 a month. The difference between what the tenant pays the landlord in rent and what is collected in sublease rent is the tenant's profit. In this case, the tenant's monthly LASH profit would be $800.

Where to Find Valid Lease Agreements

The term *valid lease agreement* refers to a lease that has been approved—usually by the real estate attorneys working for a professional association—for use in your state. You want to always use a valid lease agreement, approved for use by a professional trade association, because it will pass legal scrutiny in court. I recommend that you buy a copy of a valid lease agreement from one of the various professional associations, which represent the owners of residential, commercial, industrial, and office properties in your state, and then modify the agreement to fit your needs. For example, when you need a valid residential lease, buy a copy from your local apartment owners' association. As far as I am concerned, the generic lease agreements, which you can buy from office supply stores or download for free from web sites on the Internet, are good for only two things: lining birdcages and wrapping garbage.

Twenty Key Provisions That Must Be Included in Your Master Lease Agreement

Please do as I told you in Chapter 5 and always use separate master lease and real estate option agreements to document your LASH transaction. Whether you buy a sample copy of a valid lease agreement from a professional association or hire a competent real estate attorney to prepare one for you, make sure that all of your master lease agreements include the following 20 key provisions:

1. Parties.
2. Agreement to lease.
3. Legal description of the property.
4. Term of the lease.
5. Holdover.
6. Lease rental rate.
7. Security deposit.
8. Services and utilities.
9. Use of premises.
10. Signs.
11. Waste, nuisance, and illegal use.
12. Maintenance, repairs, and alterations.
13. Entry and inspection.
14. Damage or destruction by fire, storms, and earthquakes.
15. Condemnation.
16. Notices.
17. Applicable law.
18. Arbitration of disputes.
19. Legal costs.
20. Execution of the lease agreement by landlord and tenant.

Thirty Key Provisions to Include in Your Sublease Agreements

Include the following provisions in all of your commercial sublease agreements:

1. Parties.
2. Agreement to sublease.

3. Legal description of the property.

4. Term of the sublease.

5. Holdover.

6. Sublease rental rate.

7. Security deposit.

8. Indemnification of lessor and sublessor.

9. Services and utilities.

10. Use of premises.

11. Signs.

12. Waste, nuisance, and illegal use.

13. Maintenance, repairs, and alterations.

14. Entry and inspection.

15. Damage or destruction by fire, war, or acts of God.

16. Condemnation.

17. Default by sublessee.

18. Termination and re-entry by sublessor on sublessee's default.

19. Default by lessor or sublessor.

20. No right to assign sublease agreement.

21. No subletting.

22. Surrender of premises and keys.

23. Disposition of fixtures and personal property upon expiration of sublease.

24. Removal of property by sublessor.

25. Sublessee's insolvency, bankruptcy receivership, or assignment for creditors.

26. Notices.

27. Applicable law.

28. Arbitration of disputes.

29. Legal costs.

30. Execution of the sublease agreement by sublessor and sublessee.

Three Ways to Best Protect Your Position as Master Lessee

Here are three ways to protect your position as master lessee during the lease period:

1. Record a memorandum of lease, like the sample in Chapter 5, to give the public constructive notice that you have a leasehold interest in the property.
2. Buy a leasehold owner's title insurance policy to insure your leasehold interests—rights of possession and use of the premises—as provided for in your master lease agreement.
3. Buy a general liability insurance policy to cover you in the event that someone files a lawsuit for alleged damages sustained while on your leased property.

Four Key Points That Must Be Negotiated in a Master Lease

When negotiating the terms of a master lease, use the negotiating techniques, tactics, and strategies that I outline in Chapter 13, and pay special attention to the following four key points:

1. *Monthly rental rate:* Negotiate a flat monthly rental rate for the entire term of the lease.
2. *The term of the lease:* Negotiate a long-term (two- to five-year) lease.
3. *The right to sublet the premises:* Negotiate the right to sublease the premises to a third party.
4. *The right to assign the lease:* Negotiate an assignment clause in the lease, which allows you to sell the master lease to a third party.

Best to Use the LASH Strategy on Small Mismanaged Rental Properties

Just as all properties are not option properties, not all properties are LASH property candidates. The LASH strategy works best on small mismanaged rental properties that:

1. Are located in stable, low-crime, moderate-income neighborhoods near large employers, military bases, schools, shopping centers, and healthcare facilities.
2. Have below-market rental rates that can be increased by at least $150 per rental unit once the property turnaround has been completed.

3. Have mismanagement problems that can be quickly and inexpensively corrected by implementing aggressive professional property management practices.

4. Are structurally sound and have deferred maintenance that can be quickly and inexpensively repaired.

5. Can be bought for at least 20 percent below market value on buyer-friendly terms with seller-financed mortgage or deed of trust loans.

The Five Main Reasons Many Rental Properties Become Mismanaged

From my experiences buying mismanaged rental properties, I have found that incompetent ownership is the number one reason that rental properties end up being mismanaged. This incompetence has a snowball effect and is the direct result of the owner's:

1. *Lack of knowledge about the local rental market, which results in rental units being rented at below-market rental rates:* This produces a breakeven cash flow, which is barely enough to pay for maintenance and debt service when the property is at 100 percent occupancy. Any vacancy causes cash flow problems that must be covered by the property owner.

2. *Lack of knowledge and professional property management skills necessary to screen and select qualified tenant applicants as customers:* This results in tenants who will not or cannot pay their rent on time and creates a negative cash flow, which the owner must subsidize from personal funds in order to keep the mortgage or deed of trust loan current.

3. *Failure to respond to tenants' routine maintenance requests in a timely manner:* This causes tenant turnover and vacancies, which increases the negative cash flow that the owner must subsidize in order to maintain the property and pay the debt service.

4. *Failure to perform routine maintenance, which results in a neglected, run-down-looking rental property, with thousands of dollars worth of deferred maintenance:* This type of property appeals only to a class of tenants known universally as tenants from hell, who are notorious for not paying their rent and being malicious vandals.

5. *Failure to initiate eviction lawsuits against the nonpaying tenants from hell:* This results in the property being taken over by the tenants from hell, which usually ends with the lender foreclosing on the mortgage or deed of trust

loan because the owner is broke from subsidizing the negative cash flow and has filed a bankruptcy petition.

The Four Types of Property Mismanagement That Affect Small Rental Properties

The four types of property mismanagement that affect many rental properties are:

1. *Tenant mismanagement:* This occurs when there are no tenant qualification standards, screening requirements, or eviction procedures in place. Tenants are selected strictly on a "first-come, first-served basis," and there is no sense of urgency when it comes to evicting tenants for nonpayment of rent.
2. *Financial mismanagement:* This happens when units are rented at below-market rental rates, there is no organized effort to collect rental payments in arrears, and there are no formal records being maintained for income and expenses.
3. *Maintenance mismanagement:* This is the result of tenant maintenance requests being deferred or botched by hapless handymen masquerading as professional repairmen and no preventive maintenance program in place.
4. *Records mismanagement:* This happens when there are no formal property, tenant, employee, and tax records being maintained for the property.

Six Telltale Signs of a Grossly Mismanaged Rental Property

You do not need to be a property management whiz to be able to quickly identify a rental property that is suffering from gross mismanagement. All you need to do is just look for the following six telltale signs of property mismanagement:

Sign 1: Property and grounds are suffering from an obvious lack of routine maintenance and are in a neglected, run-down condition.

Sign 2: Tenant turnover and vacancy rates are abnormally high.

Sign 3: Unregistered and non-operable vehicles are conspicuously parked on the grounds.

Sign 4: Uncollected rental payments are more than 30 days in arrears.

Sign 5: Rental units are damaged as a result of tenant negligence and vandalism.

Sign 6: Property, tenant, income and expense, and tax records are either in total disarray or non-existent.

My Favorite Type of LASH Property

My favorite type of LASH property is a small (2- to 12-unit) mismanaged residential rental property, which is made of masonry (cinder block) construction and has single-story, side-by-side, separate-metered rental units with off-street parking. I specialize in this type of LASH property for the following five reasons:

1. Rental properties made of masonry construction are pretty much immune to the termites, dry rot, moisture intrusion, cracking, warping, and shrinking that generally affect wood frame construction. And, masonry exterior surfaces are easier and cheaper to clean, prep, repair, and paint than wooden exteriors.

2. Single-story rental units are easier and cheaper to maintain than two-story properties, and they are more appealing to tenants who prefer not to have someone living above or below them. Plus, you do not have the added worry that careless tenants will flood out the units below them.

3. Side-by-side rental units eliminate tenant common areas, which can be costly and time consuming to maintain and can pose a potential security and liability risk.

4. Separate-metered rental units make tenants financially responsible for their own water, sewage, trash removal, electric, and gas utility payments. This eliminates the high costs associated with providing utilities to tenants who have no incentive to conserve and who want to get their money's worth when it comes to water and electricity when the landlord is picking up the tab.

5. Small rental properties that are located in older neighborhoods and provide off-street parking are in demand because parking a car overnight on a narrow street can be risky at best.

When I find a small mismanaged residential rental property that meets my LASH property criteria, I negotiate a two-year real estate option and a two-year, flat-rate master lease, with a fixed monthly master lease payment, which is based on the property's monthly mortgage payment. For example, my last LASH property was a run-down six-unit building with a monthly loan payment of $1,600, which included principal, interest, taxes, and insurance, and that is what I agreed to pay in monthly master lease payments. When I took over the property, each two-bedroom, one-bathroom unit was rented for $400, and all of the tenants were on month-to-month leases. Two years later, when I sold my option for a $25,000 profit, all of the units were rented for $550 to tenants who were on 12-month leases. During the two years that I controlled the property, I increased its annual gross income by $7,200, which I used to clean and fix up the place. And I was still able to put $6,000 in my pocket! For complete information on how to turn a small mismanaged rental property around, I recommend that you read my book, *How to Find, Buy, and Turn Around Small Mismanaged Rental Properties for Maximum Profit*, which is available for purchase at my web site, www.thomaslucier.com.

The Four Key Functions of Property Management

There really is nothing complicated about managing residential and commercial tenants. You do not need 100 hours of dry, dull, boring property management courses or 10 years of property management experience in order to be an effective property manager. As far as I am concerned, property management can be best summed up in these four words: select, collect, maintain, and administer. All that you really need to know to be a competent property manager is how to:

1. *Select* the best qualified tenant applicants available.
2. *Collect* rental payments on the day they are due, or initiate eviction proceedings.
3. *Maintain* the property in an efficient, clean, safe, and cost-effective manner.
4. *Administer* accurate income, expense, tenant, property, and tax records.

The landlords who quickly learn how to master the tenant selection, rent collection, property maintenance, and record administration aspects of the property rental business are the ones who are profitable and stay in business. They are also the ones who quickly come to the realization that the term *property management* is a misnomer and that they are really in the people management business. There are a lot of little tricks of the landlord trade that you need to know in order to avoid being taken to the cleaners by the numerous professional deadbeat tenants, who are experts at bilking amateur landlords out of free rent and unpaid property damages. I have three pieces of sage advice that I would like to share with you on how to effectively manage your tenants. My first piece of advice is that you read and become familiar with your state's residential and nonresidential landlord and tenant acts. Both of these statutes are part of your state's civil statutes, which should be available online or at your county's public law library. Once you have found the statutes online, bookmark them on your computer. My second piece of advice is that you visit my award-winning web site, www.floridalandlord.com, and bookmark it on your computer for future reference. My third piece of advice is that you get your hands on a copy of my book, *The Florida Landlord's Manual,* which is available for purchase at my web site, www.thomaslucier.com, and use it as your hands-on guide to running a profitable, hassle-free rental property business. Ignore the specific reference to Florida because 95 percent of the book's content is applicable to do-it-yourself landlords nationwide.

Six Steps You Must Follow to Avoid Renting to the Proverbial Tenant from Hell

Face it: America is overpopulated with board-certified, repeat-offender tenants from hell, who specialize in bilking ignorant, unsuspecting landlords out of millions of dollars in unpaid rent and property damage annually. Here are six steps that you must follow when selecting tenant applicants to avoid being victimized by the numerous tenants from hell:

Step 1: Establish tenant qualification standards based on legitimate business reasons.

Step 2: Provide all tenant applicants with a copy of your tenant qualification standards.

Step 3: Apply your tenant qualification standards uniformly to all tenant applicants.

Step 4: Require consumer credit and criminal background reports on all tenant applicants.

Step 5: Check, verify, and evaluate the rental history and income of all tenant applicants.

Step 6: Deny rent to all tenant applicants who do not meet your tenant qualification standards.

Tenant Selection Is the Most Important Aspect of the Rental Property Business

The number one reason for landlord failure in America is lax or non-existent tenant screening procedures. And that is exactly why tenant selection is the single most important aspect of the entire rental property business. Tenants who are mature, conscientious, civilized, and financially responsible adults are the lifeblood of any profitable rental property business. The only practical way for a landlord to ensure that he or she selects only mature, conscientious, civilized, financially responsible adults as tenants is to screen out immature, uncivilized, financially irresponsible, management-intensive people. When landlords fail to properly screen all of their tenant applicants, they lose control of not only their tenants but also their rental property, which often results in foreclosure and bankruptcy. The first step in the tenant screening process is to establish tenant qualification standards, which are based on legitimate business reasons and not personal prejudices. Once standards are set, they must be applied uniformly to all tenant applicants. At a minimum, all tenant applicants should be required to meet the following 10 qualification standards:

1. *Complete and sign a rental application:* All tenant applicants must legibly and truthfully complete and sign a rental application.

2. *Complete and sign a release of personal information form:* All tenant applicants must legibly and truthfully complete and sign a release of personal information form, which authorizes the landlord or landlord's agent to obtain personal information about the applicant's credit, criminal, rental, and employment history.

3. *Pay a nonrefundable cash rental application fee:* All tenant applicants must pay a nonrefundable, cash rental application fee to have their application processed.

4. *Be 18 years of age:* All tenant applicants must be 18 years of age. In most states, the legal age of consent to enter into binding written agreements is 18. If you enter into a rental agreement with a minor under the legal age of 18, the agreement will be unenforceable in court.

5. *Possess valid personal photo identification:* All tenant applicants must have a valid form of personal photo identification, such as a state-issued driver's license, state-issued identification card, U.S. Department of Defense identification card, or U.S. passport or visa. Do not rent to tenant applicants who do not have a valid form of personal photo identification to prove who they are.

6. *Be a legal resident of the United States:* All tenant applicants must be legal residents of the United States. Do not rent to tenant applicants who cannot provide proof through valid photo identification that they are legal residents of the United States. Please note that it is a crime to rent to illegal aliens.

7. *Have a good credit history:* All tenant applicants must be creditworthy and have no charged-off accounts, accounts placed for collection, late payment

accounts, or bankruptcy within the past 24 months. Do not rent to tenant applicants with lousy credit histories.

8. *Have no violent or repeat nonviolent criminal conviction history:* All tenant applicants must have no violent criminal convictions and no nonviolent criminal convictions within the past seven years. Do not rent to tenant applicants who have violent criminal convictions or nonviolent criminal convictions.

9. *Have a good rental history:* All tenant applicants must have a rental history with no late payments, evictions, or judgments for past-due rent. Do not rent to tenant applicants with lousy rental histories.

10. *Have a verifiable source of legitimate and sufficient income:* All tenant applicants must have a verifiable source of legitimate income equal to three times their monthly rental rate. Tenant applicants who have no legitimate means of support may be involved in criminal activity. Do not rent to tenant applicants who cannot provide a verifiable source of legitimate income equal to three times their monthly rental rate.

Thoroughly Screen All Tenant Applicants

You must thoroughly screen all tenant applicants uniformly in order to avoid renting to immature, uncivilized, financially irresponsible, and management-intensive people, better known as tenants from hell! The best way to weed out potentially undesirable tenants is to check, verify, and evaluate their:

1. Credit history.
2. Criminal history.
3. Rental history.
4. Income.

The best way to avoid unwittingly renting to professional deadbeats and career criminals is to obtain consumer and business credit and criminal background reports on all tenant applicants to check, verify, and evaluate their credit and criminal histories. Contact the following credit reporting agencies to obtain credit and criminal background reports on tenant applicants:

Equifax Credit Information Services: www.equifax.com

Trans Union, LLC: www.transunion.com

Experian Consumer Credit Services: www.experian.com

Dunn & Bradstreet Business Information Reports: www.dnb.com

Experian Business Profile Reports: www.experian.com

To help defray the cost of screening tenant applicants, I recommend that you collect a nonrefundable cash rental application fee from all applicants when they submit their rental application. Make certain that you never process a rental application without first collecting the appropriate nonrefundable cash application fee upfront.

You Must Base Your Denial to Rent on Legitimate Business Reasons

After you have used credit and criminal background reports and other sources to check, verify, and evaluate a tenant applicant's personal and business information, you must decide to accept or deny the applicant based solely on whether he or she is a good business risk and not on personal prejudices. The following are four examples of legitimate business reasons to deny rent to tenant applicants:

1. *Credit history:* People who do not pay their bills are a bad business risk.
2. *Criminal history:* People who have been convicted of crimes are a bad business risk.
3. *Rental history:* People who do not pay their rent or have been evicted are a bad business risk.
4. *Income:* People with no verifiable source of legitimate income or insufficient income are a bad business risk.

Finally, deny rent to all tenant applicants who do not meet all of your tenant qualification standards, regardless of whether they are members of any government-protected class of tenants. If you do make *any* exceptions to your stated tenant qualification standards, you will be in direct violation of the Fair Housing Act for singling out certain groups of people for special treatment, which is the very definition of discrimination.

PART III

A 12-STEP PROCESS FOR BUYING AND RESELLING REAL ESTATE OPTIONS

How to Use the Internet, Property Wanted Ads, Bird Dogs, Finder's Fees, and Direct Mail to Locate Properties to Put under Option

In the first eight chapters of this book, I gave you the lowdown on how real estate options work and told you about money-making option strategies that you can use to profit from undervalued properties, with immediate resale profit potential. In this chapter, you will learn the details of how to go about finding properties to buy options on. However, if you expect to find potentially profitable option properties conveniently listed in the classified ad section of your local newspaper under real estate options for sale, you are in for a big disappointment. The same holds true if you expect to drive around town and find properties sprouting real estate option for sale signs. This is just not the way that it works in this business. Why not? Because the most potentially profitable types of properties to buy real estate options on are usually not widely advertised or, in many cases, are not even for sale. This means that when you go on the prowl for option properties, you will have to search them out. And to do this, you will need to be part bloodhound and part sleuth. But finding undervalued properties to buy real estate options on takes a lot more than just being a good gumshoe; it also takes a detailed property search plan, a lot of hard work, dogged determination, timing, and a certain element of luck.

My Real Estate Option Investment Business Modus Operandi

My real estate option investment business consists of one person, me. I work alone and have no hourly employees at my beck and call. And, I love running my real estate investment business this way! When I need to have something done, I hire it out to an independent contractor, who charges me by the job. By doing this, I avoid all of the rigmarole that goes along with babysitting hourly employees and dealing with the numerous government agencies that oversee employers. Because of my business modus operandi and the plain fact that I am what most people would consider downright frugal, I have to use inexpensive property search methods that do not require my physical presence in order to be effective, but which allow me to be at the right place at the right time. I accomplish this by:

1. Using the Internet, web sites, and uniform resource locator (URL) forwarding in my constant search for potentially profitable properties that I can buy low-cost real estate options on.
2. Placing classified property wanted ads in daily newspapers.
3. Mailing letters to out-of-town and problem property owners.
4. Obtaining insider information on potential option properties that are not advertised from my own network of paid informants, commonly known as *bird dogs*.
5. Paying finder's fees to people who tell me about properties that I buy options on.
6. Keeping a constant lookout during my daily travels for vacant, run-down properties that are potential option properties.

The Most Important Advice in This Entire Chapter

Here is the most important advice in this entire chapter: When searching for undervalued properties to buy real estate options on, concentrate all of your efforts on identifying, locating, and contacting the owners of property in your area who are most likely to sell you a real estate option on their property. In most areas, this means honing in on out-of-town and problem property owners. Why these two particular types of owners? In most cases, out-of-town and problem property owners have a compelling personal or financial reason for wanting to sell their property. As a result, they are the type of property owners who will provide you with the most opportunities to buy low-cost real estate options on properties that you can purchase at below-market prices. If you follow the advice I am giving you here, you will be able to find profitable option properties in half the time that it will take most other people who are clueless about where to look. However, if you completely ignore what I have just told you to do and instead look for properties to buy options on in the usual helter-skelter fashion employed by most people, you will more than likely come up empty-handed. And all you'll have done is squandered away your valuable time and money.

Develop an Aggressive Five-Pronged Property Search Plan

To beat your competitors to the most profitable option properties in town and to avoid being eaten alive by the bottom-feeding sharks in your real estate market, you need to develop an aggressive property search plan that involves the following five property search methods:

1. The Internet.
2. Property wanted ads.
3. Bird dogs.
4. Finder's fees.
5. Direct mail.

How to Locate All of the Out-of-Town Property Owners in Your County

Most out-of-town or absentee property owners become that way because they either inherited a property or, for whatever reason, were forced to relocate and failed to sell their property before they left town. Or, the property is owned by a business entity such as a corporation or limited liability company located outside the county. How do you know if a property belongs to an out-of-town or absentee owner? Simply check the property owner's post office mailing address listed for the parcel on your county's property tax roll. If the owner's mailing address is out of your county, then the property belongs to an out-of-town owner. And the farther out-of-town owners live, the better your chances are of being able to buy a low-cost real estate option on their property. I suggest that you contact the customer service department at your county property appraiser or assessor's office to see if they maintain a database of property owners residing outside the county. If not, ask if they know of a private company that maintains a database of the county's real property ownership records. However, *do not* resort to using the so-called shotgun mailing method to contact out-of-town property owners. The shotgun mailing method refers to contacting every property owner on a mailing list, regardless of the property's location or physical condition. Instead of sending a letter to every out-of-town property owner in your county, I recommend that you use zip codes to determine which owners to mail letters to. This way, you can target the owners of properties that are located in the areas you feel comfortable investing in. The following two companies maintain real property ownership record databases:

1. First American Real Estate Solutions: www.firstamres.com/html/home.asp
2. DataQuick: www.dataquick.com

In my county, I can order customized property data on CD-ROM from the Hillsborough County Property Appraiser's office. The property data is broken down by Florida Department of Revenue (DOR) land use or zoning codes and costs $60 per code designation. For example, I recently bought a CD-ROM containing property data for all of the parcels in Hillsborough County that are designated DOR land use code 08, which denotes multifamily properties with fewer than 10 units. I requested the following data on parcels belonging to owners residing outside the county:

1. Parcel's street address.
2. Owner's mailing address.
3. Parcel's assessed value.

How to Use a Property Wanted Web Page to Search for Properties Online

First and foremost, use what I commonly refer to as the great equalizer, the Internet, to search online for properties to buy real estate options on. The most efficient way I know of doing this is to have a property wanted web page on your web site, which uses URL forwarding for a property wanted domain name. If you already have an existing web site online, for an annual fee of around $50, you can have your property wanted domain name forwarded to a specific web page on your web site. For example, when you use URL forwarding, or domain redirection, you can link your property wanted domain name directly to a property wanted web page on your existing web site. This way, you avoid the cost and aggravation of building an entirely new web site for your property wanted domain name. For example, my company, Home Equities Corp, owns the URL or domain name www.rentalpropertywanted.com, which has URL forwarding to the property wanted web page at www.homeequitiescorp.com. This means that whenever the domain name www.rentalpropertywanted is typed into a browser, the URL is automatically forwarded to the Home Equities Corp web site, which is the destination domain.

Link Your Property Wanted Web Page to Other Web Sites

I also recommend that you link your property wanted web page to other web sites that you or your friends and business associates own. For example, on my web site, www.floridalandlord.com, there is a Tampa Rental Property Wanted button, which is linked to the Home Equities Corp property wanted web page. By doing this, I am placing an online property wanted ad right under the nose of all of the residential rental property owners in the Tampa Bay area who visit www.florida-landlord.com and want to sell their property. All they have to do is click on the Tampa Rental Property Wanted button and follow the instructions to submit their property for consideration.

How to Use Classified Property Wanted Ads to Find Potential Option Properties

Over the years, I have had pretty good success using classified property wanted ads to find non-advertised problem properties to buy real estate options on. Most people call me because they do not have the time, desire, or money to market their properties themselves. Or, they do not want to go through the hassle of listing their property with a real estate broker. Sure, I have received my fair share of calls from flakes, loonies, and other assorted crazies. But I have been willing to put up with the hassle and inconvenience because I have usually found the type of property that I was advertising for. When writing your classified property wanted ad, use as few words as possible to get your message across. Nowadays, most papers have a four-line minimum, with each line consisting of no more than 26 characters. To keep your ad right at four lines, write it out on graph paper, which comes already divided into small squares. By doing this, you will avoid wasting time dilly-dallying around trying to lay out your ad. What is the secret to getting your phone to ring off the hook with people calling in response to your classified property wanted ad? It is all in how your ad is written. To be effective, your ad needs to do the following three things:

1. Get the attention of the property owners who are most likely to sell you a real estate option on their property.

2. Arouse the interest of property owners as to what you may be willing to offer them for their property.

3. Motivate property owners to call and tell you about any properties they may be willing to sell real estate options on.

The Best Place to List Your Property Wanted Ad

To ensure that you get the best possible response from your classified property wanted ad, place it in the classified real estate section, under various headings such as:

1. Investment property wanted.

2. Income property wanted.

3. Commercial property wanted.

4. Property wanted.

5. Real estate wanted.

When to Run Your Property Wanted Ad

When is the best time to run your classified property wanted ad? To find out, you will have to experiment by running your ad on various days to find out what works best in your area. For example, in Tampa, I run one of my property wanted ads only in the Sunday edition of the *Tampa Tribune*. I found that I get pretty much the same response whether I run the same ad for 30 consecutive days or just on Sundays. In addition, I save a small fortune in advertising costs. The kind of response that you will get from your classified property wanted ad depends on four things:

1. How well your ad is written.

2. The classified heading under which it is placed.

3. The size of the paper's circulation.

4. What you say in your ad.

Here is an example of an actual property wanted ad with a forwarded domain name, which my company, Home Equities Corp, has run in the Florida regional edition of the *Wall Street Journal* under Real Estate Wanted:

Tampa Rentals Wanted!

I Buy Problem Properties.

All Situations Considered.

Principals Only, Please!

Rentalpropertywanted.com

tjlucier@homeequitiescorp.com

The following copy of my business card, which I use as a small display ad and e-mail to property owners who call or e-mail me about my property wanted ads:

Fourteen Questions to Ask Owners Calling about Your Property Wanted Ads

Here are 14 standard questions that you need to ask every property owner calling in response to your classified property wanted ads:

1. Where is the property located? _____

2. Who owns the property? _____

3. What condition is the property in? _____

4. Is the property currently occupied? ( ) Yes ( ) No

5. Does the property have a first mortgage loan? ( ) Yes ( ) No

6. What type of first mortgage loan does it have? ( ) Conventional ( ) Private

7. How much is owed on the first mortgage loan? _____

8. Does the property have a second mortgage loan? ( ) Yes ( ) No

9. How much is owed on the second mortgage loan? _____

10. Are the mortgage loan payments current? ( ) Yes ( ) No

11. Are there any liens other than the mortgage against the property? ( ) Yes ( ) No

12. How long have you owned the property? _____

13. Is the property tax payment current? ( ) Yes ( ) No

14. How much do you want for your equity in the property? _____

How to Use Bird Dogs to Find Potential Option Properties That Are Not Advertised

A bird dog is someone who comes into frequent contact with problem property owners within a specific neighborhood or area and is in a position to learn about non-advertised potential option properties that are for sale there. These types of hidden properties are never formally advertised as being for sale; their availability is made known only by word-of-mouth. A neighbor, a relative, or an acquaintance may be the only one who knows of a property owner's willingness or need to sell. Once you recruit these types of people into your bird dog network of paid informants, you will be in a position to receive valuable insider information on non-advertised potential option properties without the general public ever knowing of their availability.

How to Recruit Bird Dogs into Your Network of Paid Informants

The best way to find bird dogs to join your network of paid informants is to tell everyone that you come into frequent contact with that you are looking to buy real estate and that you are willing to pay a finder's fee when you buy an option on a property that they told you about. Here is a listing of the types of people you want to recruit into your network as bird dogs:

1. Mail carriers.
2. Trash collectors.
3. Doctors.
4. Dentists.
5. Employees.
6. Fellow club members.
7. Fellow church members.
8. Door-to-door salespeople.
9. Delivery truck drivers.
10. Tradesmen.
11. Repair men.
12. Business colleagues.
13. Coworkers.
14. Neighbors.
15. Friends.
16. Tenants.
17. Taxicab drivers.
18. Utility meter readers.

Pay a Finder's Fee for Information That Results in the Purchase of an Option

The best way that I have found to motivate people to contact me with valuable information on non-advertised problem properties is to offer to pay a finder's fee to anyone who tells me about a property that I put under option. For example, my standard finder's fee is $500 cash, payable on the same day that I buy the real estate option. I pay $500 because it seems to be the figure that gets the attention of most people. I use to offer $300, but since I have upped the ante to $500, I have more than doubled the number of leads that I get monthly from people calling to tell me about various problem properties. The thing that I like best about paying finder's fees is that I have to pay them only when I buy a real estate option. In the meantime, I have the benefit of a lot of people looking for properties for me without the cost of a weekly payroll. I know an option investor in Orange County, California, who specializes in buying options on properties that have been stigmatized by being the scenes of violent crimes. To find these types of properties, this investor has enlisted the help of the technicians who work for the companies that specialize in the grisly job of cleaning up crime scenes. This guy pays a $500 finder's fee for every property he buys an option on.

Use the Internet to Advertise Your Finder's Fee Online

On my real estate investment company's web site, www.homeequitiescorp.com, on the property wanted web page, there is a $500 Cash Reward button that visitors can click on to learn about how they can earn a finder's fee of $500 in cash by simply contacting me with information that results in the purchase of a dirty, neglected, run-down 2- to 12-unit residential rental property in the Tampa Bay area. I also have my $500 cash reward printed on the back of my business cards. A copy of my online message follows:

$500 Cash Reward

Home Equities Corp will pay a **$500** cash reward for information resulting in the purchase of a dirty, neglected, run-down two to twelve-unit residential rental property in the Tampa Bay Area.

That's right, when you call or e-mail us about a run-down two to twelve-unit rental property in the Tampa Bay Area, and we buy it, we'll give you **$500** cash on the day we close on the purchase . . . no games, gimmicks, or bullshot about it!

We don't care how dirty and run-down the property looks, or even if it's totally vacant. If you know where there is a property like this in the Tampa Bay Area, please call us today at **(813) 237-6267** or e-mail us at acquisitions@homeequitiescorp.com. Remember, the sooner you contact us, the sooner you get your **$500** cash reward! **NOTE:** Our $500 cash reward does not apply to properties that are listed with real estate brokers or to owners with properties for sale.

Use Direct Mail to Contact Potential
Option Property Owners

When properly used, direct mail is a quick, efficient, and relatively cost-effective way for you to make direct contact with all of the out-of-town and problem property owners in your area. Why just contact out-of-town and problem property owners? Many out-of-town and problem property owners are uninformed and out of touch when it comes to local property values. Here are four very good reasons I use direct mail to contact potential option property owners:

1. *Direct mail is easy to use.* All I have to do is sit at my computer, point and click, hit a couple of keys, and it will crank out one of my standard letters to problem property owners, which just needs to be signed, folded, and inserted into an envelope. I use Microsoft Word 2003 that can merge names and addresses with letters. I use window envelopes so I do not have to take additional time addressing them.

2. *Direct mail is relatively cheap to use.* I am a penny pincher, and direct mail is cost efficient. For example, I can mail out 100 letters first-class mail for right around $60. This includes the cost of letterheads, envelopes, and postage—the whole shebang.

3. *Direct mail is quick.* I usually get responses from owners who are interested in selling within two weeks from the date I mailed the letters.

4. *Direct mail is effective.* It allows me to make direct contact with problem property owners without having to go through third parties such as real estate agents.

What You Should Say in Your
Letter to Potential Option Property Owners

Your letter to potential option property owners should be relatively short, sweet, and to the point. There is no need to delve into the mechanics of a real estate option transaction. Doing so will only further complicate the issue and will most likely make your real estate option proposal more confusing to the property owner. If the property looks especially bad, you might want to enclose a photo or two along with your letter. Doing this will sometimes enhance your chances of getting a response, once the owner gets a glimpse of the property in its current condition. Your letter to potential option property owners should cover the following seven points:

1. The full legal name of the person or business entity making the proposal.
2. The amount of the option fee to be paid.
3. The length of the option period.
4. The purchase price of the property.
5. The amount of the down payment to be paid.
6. The method by which the purchase is to be financed.
7. The method by which to contact you.

A sample letter of proposal appears on page 93.

Always Be on the Lookout for Vacant Properties

Finally, in addition to using all five of the property search methods that I have outlined in this chapter, always be on the lookout for vacant properties while driving around town. How do you go about spotting vacant properties with profit potential? It is really not that hard to do once you know exactly what to look for. Probably the easiest and quickest way is to simply look for properties exhibiting any of the following telltale signs of blatant neglect. Look for properties that have:

1. Trash-strewn grounds.
2. Overgrown landscaping.
3. Graffiti-covered walls.
4. Broken windows.
5. Missing doors.
6. Peeling paint.
7. Leaky roofs.
8. Overgrown walkways and parking areas.

A sample letter to vacant property owners is shown on page 94.

FORM 9.1   Sample Letter of Proposal to Purchase a Real Estate Option

---

August 28, 2005

Mr. David D. Jones
5300 West Oklahoma Avenue
Tampa, FL 33629

Dear Mr. Jones,

I propose to purchase a real estate option on the property that you own at 7809 Iowa Avenue in Tampa, Florida, under the following terms:

1. I will buy a one-year real estate option to purchase your property in as is condition, for an option fee of three thousand dollars ($3,000), which will be credited towards the purchase price when the real estate option is exercised.

    Please note that the three thousand dollar ($3,000) option fee is yours to keep, whether or not I exercise the real estate option and buy your property. In other words, the $3,000 option fee is yours, whether I buy your property or not!

2. When the real estate option is exercised, I will purchase your property for one hundred thousand dollars ($100,000), and close on the purchase within 30 days.

3. When the real estate option is exercised, I will make a total down payment of six thousand dollars ($6,000), which will include a three thousand dollar ($3,000) credit, for the real estate option fee paid.

4. When the real estate option is exercised, you agree to take back a purchase money first mortgage in the approximate amount of ninety-four thousand dollars ($94,000), at an 8 percent annual percentage rate, with monthly loan payments based on a 30-year amortization period, and a balloon loan payment for the unpaid balance, due 10 years from the loan's origination date.

If you are interested in my proposal to purchase a real estate option on your property, please call me at (813) 237-6267 or e-mail me at tjlucier@tampabay.rr.com, to setup a meeting to discuss my proposal in greater detail.

Sincerely,

Thomas J. Lucier

FORM 9.2   Sample Letter to Vacant Property Owners

August 28, 2005

Mr. David D. Jones
5300 West Oklahoma Avenue
Tampa, FL 33629

Dear Mr. Jones,

I specialize in buying properties in the Tampa Bay area with title problems, ownership problems, management problems, vacancy problems, financial problems, maintenance problems, tenant problems, cash flow problems, structural problems and code violation problems.

If your property is currently experiencing similar problems, and you are interested in possibly selling, please feel free to call me anytime at (813) 237-6267 or e-mail me at tjlucier@tampabay.rr.com to discuss your situation.

If your property fits my needs, and we are able to agree on a sale price and terms, I will be able to close on the purchase within 10 business days or less, depending upon your particular circumstance.

I look forward to hearing from you soon and to helping you solve your property problems.

Sincerely,

Thomas J. Lucier

CHAPTER 10

How to Perform Due Diligence on a Potential Option Property

Over the past 24 years, my real property research credo has evolved into: Trust no one, assume nothing, verify everything, and be prepared for anything! I have learned the hard way not to automatically assume that all of the information contained in the official public records about a property is complete, up-to-date, and 100 percent accurate. It usually is not. The only way to obtain reliable, up-to-date information on a property and its owner is to go directly to the source of the information and then verify it, which is exactly what due diligence is all about. The purpose for performing due diligence on a potential option property is to gather the most up-to-date and verifiable information available in order to make an informed option buying decision. And, given the Internet and the vast amount of property-related information that is readily available online today, there is absolutely no valid excuse for anyone not to perform due diligence on potential option properties before they plunk down their hard-earned money to buy a real estate option. But what I really like most about using the Internet to do research on properties is that I am free to snoop around online in the comfort and privacy of my own home-based office without ever having to deal with the snotty clerks that are all too prevalent in government offices today. In today's wired world, computer-savvy option investors can quickly perform most of their property due diligence research by using their personal computer and an Internet connection linking them to the myriad of web sites that contain information on a property's:

1. Ownership.
2. Liens.
3. Sales history.
4. Tax assessed value.

5. Environmental hazards.
6. Crime rate.
7. Demographic information.

The Definition of Due Diligence

In general legal terms, *due diligence* is defined as: "The care that a reasonable, prudent person exercises in the examination and evaluation of risks affecting a business transaction."

How to Use the Internet to Perform Due Diligence Research on Properties

I do not know about you, but as far as I am concerned, the Internet is one of the greatest inventions of all time and ranks right up there with flush toilets, incandescent light bulbs, and air conditioning! For real estate investors, the Internet is the single best property due diligence research tool available, especially for investors who are located in counties where the property tax rolls are available online. And if your county's property records are available online, you can quickly find out who owns a property, when it was purchased, how much it cost, and its tax-assessed value. For example, here in Tampa, I can log on to the Hillsborough County Property Appraiser's web site and, armed only with a property's street address, I can almost instantly obtain the current owner's name, mailing address, sale price, and dates for the latest and prior sales and the tax-assessed value of the property broken down by land and improvements. I can also get a site map plotting the improvements on the property, along with the tax account or folio number assigned to the property. Then, I log on to the Hillsborough County Tax Collector's web site and type in the property's street address or tax folio number to obtain property tax information about the property to include any tax exemptions claimed, special tax-district assessments, and tax payment status. Once I have completed my online research, I call the customer service departments at the property appraiser and tax collector's offices to verify the accuracy of the information they have posted online.

Be Sure to Check Out the Owner When Performing Due Diligence on the Property

Do not make the mistake that most investors make when they perform due diligence on a property and fail to check out the owner at the same time. I like to know as much about a property owner's physical, emotional, legal, mental, and financial condition as I do about the physical and financial condition of the property under consideration for purchase. The reason I want to do the equivalent of a strip search on property owners is to find out if there are any outside factors, such as bankruptcy, engagement, divorce, death, arrest, criminal charges, and imprisonment, that could influence a property owner's decision-making process. Case in point: Last year I was able to buy a two-year option on a vacant, run-down, rail-front warehouse that is worth well over $500,000 for only $5,000 with a fixed purchase price of $375,000. I was able to negotiate a low-cost option and a below-market purchase price because I had done my homework on the elderly owner and found out by reading a newspaper article that he was engaged to be married to a prominent socialite and was going to be cutting back on his workload and unloading some of the properties in his portfolio. And because I had taken the time and effort to learn about the owner's personal situation, I was able to strike a deal with him for the warehouse.

Why You Should Do a Google Search of the Property Owner's Name

Google is my favorite Internet search engine of all time. And nowadays, as part of my standard due diligence procedure, I always enter the property owner's name into the Google search engine and wait to see what pops up on my computer screen. I remember finding out about one owner who had recently lost a specific performance lawsuit, in which he had defaulted on a real estate purchase agreement by failing to sell the property as agreed. After reading about this unscrupulous owner's exploits in court documents, I decided to pass on the property.

Best to Use the Checklist Method When Performing Property Due Diligence Research

I can trace my fondness for checklists back to my days as a Marine Corps recruit at Parris Island, South Carolina, where checklists were used extensively by drill instructors to keep track of everything from weapons to bedsheets. And from that time on, I have been hooked on checklists! As far as I am concerned, the checklist method is the fastest and most efficient way to perform the following due diligence searches on potential option properties:

1. *Property records search:* Check your county property appraiser or assessor's property records for ownership, sale, and tax assessment information.

2. *Property tax records search:* Check your county tax collector's property tax records for tax payment information.

3. *Comparable sales search:* Check your county's property records for recent sales of comparable properties during the past six months.

4. *Neighborhood crime search:* Check the crime risk rating for the property's address with local law enforcement agencies.

5. *Flood zone map search:* Check the property's address on federal flood maps to determine whether it is located in a flood zone.

6. *Hazardous waste search:* Check the property's address for environmental hazards with local, state, and federal environmental protection agencies.

7. *Demographic data search:* Check demographic data for the property's address with local state and federal agencies.

8. *Code violation search:* Check the property's address for code violations with your local code enforcement department.

Environmental Hazardous Waste Search Online

To perform an environmental hazardous waste search on a potential option property, log on to the following web sites:

EPA superfund hazardous waste site search: www.epa.gov/superfund/sites /query/basic.htm

Environmental hazards zip code search: www.scorecard.org

EPA Enviromapper zip code search: www.epa.gov/cgi-bin/enviro/em/empact /getZipCode.cgi?appl=empact&info=zipcode

HUD environmental maps: www.hud.gov/offices/cio/emaps/index.cfm

Demographic Information Online

The following is a listing of online sources of demographic information:

FFIEC Geocoding System: www.ffiec.gov/geocode/default.htm

U.S. Census Bureau FactFinder: www.factfinder.census.gov/servlet /BasicFactsServlet

U.S. Census Bureau Gazetteer: www.census.gov/cgi-bin/gazetteer

U.S. Census Bureau QuickFacts: www.quickfacts.census.gov/qfd/index.html

U.S. Census Bureau zip code statistics: www.census.gov/epcd/www/zipstats
.html

Business Information Solutions demographic data by zip code: www.infods
.com/freedata

Crime Statistics Online

The following is a listing of sources of online crime statistics nationwide:

Crime.com: www.crime.com/info/crime_stats/crime_stats.html

Neighborhood crime check: www.apbnews.com/resourcecenter/datacenter
/index.html

Where to Find the Names of All the Property Owners in Your County

The name of virtually every property owner in your county is available at your county property appraiser or assessor's office on what's known as the property tax roll. The property tax roll lists every parcel of land in a given county. Depending on where you live, each parcel is assigned a separate tax identification number, either an assessor's parcel number (APN) or an appraiser's folio number. To find out if your county's property tax roll is available online, simply type the name of your county and state into an Internet search engine, such as www.google.com, and click on search. Be aware that in so-called nondisclosure states, only the principals and any real estate licensees involved in a real estate transaction know the sale price. The sale prices of real estate transactions aren't publicly disclosed in the following six nondisclosure states:

1. Indiana.
2. Kansas.
3. Mississippi.
4. New Mexico.
5. Utah.
6. Wyoming.

If you live in a nondisclosure state, you will have to get sales data from a private company that maintains real property ownership records for your county or from real estate licensees who have access to the local multiple listing service records. The following is a listing of web sites of companies that maintain real property ownership record databases:

First American Real Estate Solutions: www.firstamres.com/html/home.asp
DataQuick: www.dataquick.com

Where to Search for Property Records Online

The following web sites list the county property appraiser and assessor offices that have their property records available online:

Public Record Finder: www.publicrecordfinder.com/property.html
Public Records Sources: www.publicrecordsources.com
Access Central: www.access-central.com
Real Estate Public Records: www.real-estate-public-records.com
Search Systems: www.searchsystems.net
Tax Assessor Database: www.pubweb.acns.nwu.edu/~cap440/assess.html
Public Records Online: www.netronline.com/public_records.htm
National Association of Counties: www.naco.org/counties/counties
Public Records USA: www.factfind.com/public.htm
International Association of Assessing Officers: www.iaao.org/1234.html
Public Records Research System: www.brbpub.com

Where to Search for People Online

The following web sites provide people locator and street address information online:

Internet Address Finder: www.iaf.net
lookupusa: www.lookupusa.com
Switchboard: www.switchboard.com
Skipease: www.skipease.com
Social Security Administration Death Index: www.ancestry.com/search/rectype/vital/ssdi/main.htm

Street Address Information: www.melissadata.com/lookups/index.htm

Reverse Telephone Directory: www.reversephonedirectory.com

What to Do When Your County's Property Records Are Not Available Online

Prior to the advent of digital files, county or public recorder's offices used only a microfiche and microfilm index system to record and maintain property title documents. Once recorded, documents were placed directly onto microfilm, with each document being assigned a reel and frame number. If your county's property records are not yet available online, contact your property appraiser or assessor's customer service department to see if they provide property record information over the telephone. In most counties, you can call your property appraiser or assessor's customer service department and give them a property's street address, and they will be able to tell you the parcel or folio number, the owner's name and mailing address if it is different from the property address, when and how much the property last sold for, and the property's current tax-assessed value. This way, you will not have to go traipsing down to your property appraiser or assessor's office every time you want to look up information on a property. However, if you do have to visit your county's property appraiser or assessor's office to look up property records, please do not be the least bit bashful about asking county employees for help! When you visit your county's government offices, explain to the so-called public servants working there that you want to do a title search on a particular property to uncover all of the encumbrances, such as mortgage or deed of trust loans along with any other liens and judgments currently placed against the title to the property. In most cases, you will be given a brief orientation on how to locate a property in the official record books and how to use microfiche machines to locate documents recorded against the property's title.

How Parcels of Land Are Identified for Property Tax Purposes

Most counties are divided into map or plat books. Each map or plat book is given a separate number, and each parcel of land is given a separate tax identification number—an APN or an appraiser's folio number. The property appraiser or assessor assigns a folio number or APN to each parcel of land in the county. These folio numbers or APNs are used to compile annual property tax assessments and generally list each parcel owner's name, mailing address, and the assessed value of both the parcel and any improvements.

How You Can Use Grantor and Grantee Indexes to Find Property Owners

When a deed is recorded, it is indexed in a grantor (seller) index and at the same time in a grantee (buyer) index. Grantor and grantee indexes are maintained in alphabetical and chronological order. They are generally alphabetized according to last and first names. Let us assume that you are trying to determine a current property owner's name, but you have only the name of the person who last sold the property and the year in which it was sold. To obtain the name of the current owner, you would use the grantor's index book for the year the title was transferred to locate the grantee's name. The grantor's index lists in alphabetical order all grantors named in documents recorded during a specific calendar year; beside each grantor's name is the name of the grantee as named in the document along with the official record book and page number where a photocopy of the recorded document can be located in the public records. The grantee index is arranged by grantee names and gives the name of the grantee and the official record book and page numbers where a photocopy of the recorded document can be found.

How to Locate the Owners of Vacant Properties

You should be able to locate the owner of a vacant property by looking up the street address on your county's real property tax roll. The tax roll will have the name of the owner of record along with the post office mailing address where the property tax bill is sent. However, sometimes the address listed on the tax roll is incorrect. When this happens, go to the following sources in the county and state of the property owner's last known address, and check the:

1. County voter registration records.
2. City and county public library patron records.
3. City and county business license records.
4. City and county jail inmate records.
5. State fishing and hunting license records.
6. State professional license records.
7. State department of motor vehicles.
8. State bar association membership records.
9. State vital statistics records.
10. State prison inmate records.
11. Federal prison inmate records.
12. Social Security Administration's Death Index.

The Two Types of Real Property Liens

Real property liens are legal claims placed against a debtor's (lienee's) real property by lenders, creditors, and government agencies (lienors) to secure payment of a debt. The two types of real property liens are:

1. *Voluntary liens:* Voluntary liens are placed against the title to real property with the owner's consent, such as mortgage or deed of trust loans.

2. *Involuntary liens:* Involuntary liens are placed against the title to real property as a result of legal action by a creditor, lender, or government agency such as federal and state income tax liens, property tax liens, and mechanics' liens.

A Lien's Priority Is Determined by the Date of Recordation and Type of Lien

A lien's priority or seniority over other liens placed against the title to the same property is determined by the date or chronological order in which it was recorded in the official records and the type of lien. For example, a mortgage or deed of trust lien recorded on August 25, 2004, would have priority over another mortgage or deed of trust lien recorded on August 28, 2004, against the same property because it would be in a first or senior position over the next lien recorded. However, in most states, property and special assessment tax liens to include liens placed against real property for unpaid governmental services have priority over previously recorded mortgage or deed of trust liens. Judgment liens, mechanics' liens, and even IRS tax liens do not have seniority over previously recorded mortgage or deed of trust liens and are considered subordinate or junior liens.

Check the Public Records to Verify That All Recorded Liens Are Uncovered

When researching any property's title information, always make certain that you check the official public records in the county where the property's deed is recorded to verify that all recorded liens placed against the property's title have been uncovered. The functions of county government offices vary from state-to-state, so contact your county government to find out which offices maintain records on real property and judgment liens. The following is a listing of where to look when searching the public records for liens that are attached to the titles of real property:

1. *County recorder or prothonotary's office:* Check the grantor and grantee or mortgagor and mortgagee indexes, federal tax lien index, public assistance liens, conditional sales contracts such as contracts for deed, agreements for deed and land sales contracts, notices of lis pendens index, writs of attachment, judgment liens such as mechanic's and materialmen's liens, and property tax liens.

2. *Clerk of the county and circuit court:* Check the defendant's judgment index, state income tax liens, state inheritance tax liens, state franchise tax liens, judgment liens, homeowners' association liens, suits to quiet title, suits for specific performance, estates of deceased persons, guardianships of minors and incompetents, termination of life estates, termination of joint tenancies, and condemnation of lands.

3. *United States Court:* Check for federal judgments such as federal tax liens and judgment liens resulting from defaults on government-guaranteed FHA, Department of Veterans Affairs (DVA), Small Business Administration (SBA), and student loans.

4. *Municipal clerk's records:* Check for liens resulting from unpaid bills for municipal services such as water and sewer services and code enforcement fines.

Sixteen Liens to Check for When Researching Titles to Real Property

The following is a listing and brief description of the 16 most common liens encumbering the title to real property:

1. *Real property tax lien:* Real property tax liens are placed against properties by local taxing authorities—city and county tax collectors—when property owners fail to pay their property taxes.

2. *Federal tax lien:* Federal tax liens are statutory liens that the IRS places against the titles of real property belonging to taxpayers who fail to pay their federal income tax.

3. *Federal judgment lien:* Federal judgment liens are liens placed against the titles of real property belonging to debtors who are in default on federally guaranteed loans, such as SBA and student guaranteed loans.

4. *Mechanic's lien:* Mechanic's liens are statutory liens that allow mechanics, contractors, materialmen, architects, surveyors, and engineers who have furnished work or materials for the improvement of real property to file a lien against the debtor's real property being worked on.

5. *Judgment lien:* Judgment liens result from lawsuits awarding monetary damages. Once recorded, a lien is placed against both the real and personal property of the debtor until the judgment is paid.

6. *Mortgage and deed of trust lien:* A mortgage or deed of trust lien is a voluntary lien created when real property is pledged as security for the repayment of a debt.

7. *State inheritance tax lien:* Most states have an inheritance tax, which is levied against the estates of deceased persons. The amount of inheritance tax owed becomes a lien against the estate.

8. *Corporate franchise tax lien:* States having a corporate franchise tax will tax corporations for the right to do business within the state. When corporations fail to pay their franchise tax, the state files a lien against any real property within the state belonging to the corporation.

9. *Bail bond lien:* A lien is created when real property is pledged as a bail bond in order to allow a person arrested on criminal charges to be released on bail pending trial.

10. *Code enforcement lien:* A lien is placed against a property's title by local code enforcement boards when a property owner has been fined for failing to correct code enforcement citations and doesn't pay the fine.

11. *Municipal lien:* A lien is placed against a property's title by local governments when a property owner fails to pay for municipal services such as water, sewage, and trash removal.

12. *Welfare lien:* A lien is placed against a property's title by state and federal government agencies when a property owner collects welfare payments that he or she is not legally entitled to.

13. *Public defender lien:* A lien is placed against a property's title by federal, state, and local governments when a property owner fails to pay for a court-appointed public defender.

14. *Marital support lien:* A lien is placed against a property's title by federal and state governments when a property owner fails to pay court-ordered marital support payments.

15. *Child support lien:* A lien is placed against a property's title by state governments when a property owner fails to make court-ordered child support payments.

16. *Homeowners' association lien:* A lien is placed against a property's title by a homeowners' association when a member fails to pay his or her homeowners' dues as per the deed to the property.

For whatever reason, some county recorders are slow to index or place recorded documents into the official public records. This can result in a recorded and valid lien not showing up during a lien search of the public records. I suggest that you ask the manager at your county or public recorder's office what the time lag is between when a document is recorded and when it is actually indexed in your county's official public records.

Because of the gap in time between when a document is recorded and when it is actually indexed or placed in the official public record, make certain that you check the lis pendens—lawsuits pending—index at the clerk of the circuit and county court or recorder's office for notices of any pending lawsuits that may be filed against the title to the property. The names of the plaintiffs and defendants in the lis pendens index are arranged in alphabetical order.

Common Abbreviations Used in Property Title Documents

The following is a listing of abbreviations commonly used in property title documents:

1. Est.—Estate
2. Et al.—And others
3. Et vir.—And husband
4. Et ux.—And wife
5. Jt.—Joint tenants
6. Qc.—Quit claim deed
7. Lov—-Gift transfer
8. Dot.—Deed of Trust
9. Grantor—Seller
10. Lt.—Lot
11. Com prop.—Community property
12. Ten in com.—Tenants In Common
13. Pcl.—Parcel
14. Tr.—Trustee
15. Sec.—Section
16. Blk—Block
17. Pt.—Part
18. Tr—Tract
19. Att.—Attachment

20. Ftl.—Federal tax lien
21. Jl.—Judgment lien
22. Ln.—Lien
23. Ml.—Mechanics lien
24. Stl.—State tax lien
25. Ttl.—Town tax lien
26. Cm.—Committee deed
27. Cn.—Conservator deed
28. Ex.—Executor deed
29. Gn.—Guardian deed
30. Mtg.—Mortgage
31. Pr Mtg.—Prior mortgage
32. Tcd.—Tax collector deed
33. Td.—Trust deed
34. Wd.—Warranty deed

The Two Most Common Types of Property Title Searches

The two most common types of property title searches are:

1. *Current owner title search:* A current owner title search, sometimes referred to as a title or property report, is a search of the public records from the date the property's title was transferred to the current owner to the present.

2. *Full title search:* A full title search involves an in-depth search of the property's chain of title from the date the current owner took title back to a maximum of 60 years.

Please note that property title searches are confined to the official public records and will not uncover any off-record risks such as forgeries, fraud, and encroachments that aren't recorded in the official public records.

Best to Hire an Experienced Title Abstractor to Perform Your Title Searches

Many option investors have gotten into serious trouble because they tried to save time and money by doing only a cursory title search without having their findings verified by an experienced title researcher or abstractor. You must understand that an uncovered, but recorded, mechanic's lien, federal tax lien, or third mortgage or deed of trust loan can come back to haunt you at a later date, usually when you are in the process of trying to sell the option on the property. Researching property title information can sometimes be very tricky, even if you know what you are doing. And this is why I highly recommend that you hire an experienced title abstractor to do a title search on a property before you buy an option. To find an experienced title abstractor in your county, log on to the following web site: Abstracters Online: www.abstractersonline.com.

What You Must Double-Check on Every Potential Option Property

When performing due diligence research on a potential option property, you should always double-check the information that you have about the property with the following government offices:

1. *Local zoning department:* Whatever you do, do not just assume that the zoning designations shown on the latest tax roll are accurate. You must always verify zoning designations with your local zoning department. For example, when I need to verify a zoning designation in Tampa, all I have to do is call the city zoning department and give them the property's tax folio number. They in turn look up the folio number on their computerized zoning maps and tell me the property's current zoning designation.

2. *Local code enforcement department:* In most areas, when properties are ordered vacated and repaired because of building, safety, or health code violations, brightly colored (usually dark red or orange) placards are conspicuously posted on the property. However, some property owners will try to conceal the fact that their property has been cited for code violations, commonly referred to as being *red-tagged.* They do this by illegally removing code violation placards from their buildings. And this is why you need to check with your local code enforcement department to verify that a property's certificate of occupancy has not been revoked because of code violations.

3. *Property tax collector's office:* Check with your county property tax collector's office to verify the property's tax payment status and to see whether any tax liens are recorded against it.

4. *City and county clerk's offices:* Check with your city or county clerk's office to see whether there are any liens recorded against a property for nonpayment of municipal services such as water, sewage, solid waste, and gas.

5. *City, county, and state environmental protection agencies.* Check with your city, county, and state environmental protection agencies to see if the property has been cited for having any type of environmentally hazardous waste on it.

Verify the Property's Insurance Claims History before You Buy an Option

I do not know how expensive insurance rates are in your neck of the woods, but here in Tampa, Florida, property and casualty insurance rates have gone through the stratosphere! This is why I always check a potential option property's casualty and property insurance claims history before I make an offer to buy a real estate option. I do this by having my insurance broker verify the property's insurance claims history through the Comprehensive Loss Underwriting Exchange (C.L.U.E.), an insurance claim history information data exchange that insurance companies use to calculate insurance premiums when underwriting policies. According to the C.L.U.E. web site, their service: "provides loss history to help insurers qualify applicants and properties for homeowner coverage and helps insurers maximize premiums and minimize expenses." You must do this to determine whether the property is insurable and if it can be insured at the prevailing market rate for similar properties within the same area. To learn more about the C.L.U.E., log on to the following web site and click on C.L.U.E. report: www.choicepoint.net.

Ten Questions You Must Ask Owners before You Ever Buy a Real Estate Option

Prior to buying a real estate option, make certain that you have the property owner sign a property disclosure statement approved for use in your state in the presence of a notary public, which asks the following 10 questions:

1. Are there any hazardous substances at, on, under, or about the property? The term *hazardous substances* shall mean and include those elements or compounds that are contained in the list of hazardous substances and toxic pollutants adopted by the U.S. Environmental Protection Agency (EPA) or under any hazardous substance laws.
2. Have any documents ever been filed in the public records that adversely affect the title to the property?
3. Are there any liens against the property for unpaid bills owed to architects, surveyors, engineers, mechanics, laborers, and materialmen?

4. Are there any actions, proceedings, judgments, bankruptcies, liens, or executions recorded among the public records or pending in the courts that would affect the title to the property?

5. Are there any unpaid taxes, claims of lien, or other matters that could constitute a lien or encumbrance against the property or any of the improvements on it?

6. Have any improvements been placed on the property in violation of applicable building codes and zoning regulations?

7. Are there ongoing legal disputes concerning the location of the boundary lines of the property?

8. Is any person or entity other than the owner presently entitled to the right to possession or in possession of the property?

9. Has the title or ownership of the property ever been disputed in a court of law?

10. Are there any unrecorded mortgages or deeds of trust and promissory notes for which the property has been pledged as collateral?

Best to Avoid Properties in Areas Perceived by the Public as Being Bad Locations

Do not, under any circumstances, buy real estate options on properties in areas that are perceived by the public as being bad locations. Keep in mind that when you buy an option on any type of property, you are also buying the neighborhood in which it is located. For example, here in Tampa, there is an area around my alma mater, the University of South Florida, that is derisively called Suitcase City and frequently featured on the local six o'clock news because of drug busts, carjacking, rapes, burglaries, and other violent crimes. Suitcase City is made up almost entirely of small residential rental properties, housing tenants who receive rental housing payment assistance under HUD's Section 8 rental program. Many of the rental properties located in Suitcase City suffer from gross mismanagement and can be bought at bargain-basement prices! However, because of the public's perception of Suitcase City as being a bad location, I have steadfastly refused to buy an option on any property located there.

Eight Factors to Consider When Performing Due Diligence on Areas to Invest In

Finally, to avoid buying an option on a property in a bad location, you need to take the time to thoroughly check out the area surrounding the property under consideration. This means understanding the political, social, and economic factors that influence property values within the area. You must consider the following eight factors when performing due diligence to select the most stable and potentially profitable areas to invest in:

1. *Age and condition of properties within the area:* Avoid areas where virtually every property is old and in a run-down, neglected physical condition. This is a telltale sign that there are hard to overcome problems affecting the area, including crime, drainage, local perception, and lack of municipal services.

2. *Storm water drainage within the area:* Avoid areas with inadequate storm water drainage systems that are susceptible to chronic flooding whenever a hard rain occurs.

3. *Perception of the area within the community:* Avoid areas that are perceived within the overall community as being the local equivalent to the South Bronx in New York City. Areas having this type of an overly negative perception are next to impossible for private individuals to overcome and are best left to the swell folks at HUD to waste our tax dollars on!

4. *Enforcement of building and zoning codes within the area:* Avoid areas where building, health, safety, and fire codes and zoning regulations are not being enforced. A lack of code and zoning enforcement is a telltale sign that an area is in rapid decline.

5. *Crime rate within the area:* Avoid areas with a high crime rate or the reputation for being crime ridden. When an area has a high crime rate, established businesses try to move out while new businesses are scared away from locating in the area.

6. *Presence of public nuisances within the area:* Avoid areas that are near stinky-smelling sewer treatment plants, meat-packing plants, or paper mills unless the properties within the area have potential for use as unattended warehouses or bulk storage facilities.

7. *Availability of municipal services within the area:* Avoid areas where hookups to municipal water and sewer lines are not readily available and relatively expensive.

8. *Traffic patterns within the area:* Avoid areas that do not have relatively easy access to main thoroughfares.

CHAPTER 11

How to Thoroughly Inspect a Property before You Buy an Option to Purchase

In Chapter 10, I gave you step-by-step instructions on how to perform due diligence on a property and its owner. In this chapter, you are going to learn how to thoroughly inspect a property to determine its physical condition before you ever shell out any money on a real estate option. The reason I am so adamant about having a property inspected before I ever plunk down any of my hard-earned money for an option is that I do not want to get bamboozled by an unscrupulous owner, who just happens to be an expert at surreptitiously masking a property's defects. At least once a week, I get a telephone call or e-mail from an investor who failed to heed the very sage advice that I am dispensing here and went ahead and blindly bought a property without the benefit of an inspection. And every time I hear the same old tale of woe about how the poor investor got swindled by some shady property owner into buying a lemon of a property needing costly and time-consuming repairs. My first, last, and only question to these people is always the same: Did you have the property inspected by a licensed professional building inspector? Invariably, the answer is always the same: "No," followed by a litany of lame excuses, ranging from, "I did not have time," to, "The owner seemed like such a nice person." I do not know about you, but I have a real hard time feeling sorry for anyone who conducts his or her business affairs in such a slipshod manner. Years ago, there was a doctrine in real estate known as *caveat emptor*, which is Latin for "buyer beware." And buyers were continually warned to be on their guard when participating in a real estate transaction. However, nowadays, in our society, where the overwhelming majority of citizens would rather play the blame game than accept responsibility for their personal actions, the concept of looking out for yourself has pretty much gone by the wayside. Well, I, for one, still apply the principle of caveat emptor whenever I am involved in any type of transaction, and unless you still believe in the tooth fairy, you, too, must thoroughly inspect any potential option property for the following:

1. Structural roof damage.
2. Sinking and cracking foundations.
3. Mold contamination.
4. Electrical, fire, and safety hazards.
5. Structural dry rot damage.
6. Water and moisture intrusion.
7. Collapsed water and sewer lines.
8. Signs of termite infestation.
9. Missing roofing material, gutters, and downspouts.
10. Rotting wood.
11. Stripped mechanical systems and missing electrical wiring.

How to Locate a Competent Building Inspector

If you lack the construction knowledge and experience needed to conduct a thorough property inspection, I highly recommend you hire a licensed professional building inspector to snoop around and inspect potential option properties for you. A word of caution: The home and building inspection profession has more than its fair share of phonies, fakes, frauds, and scam artists. I attribute this problem to the fact that most states do not have any licensing requirements whatsoever for home or building inspectors. For example, in Florida, anyone can become a home inspector, simply by obtaining a city or county occupational business license. The best advice that I can give you is to use an inspector who is a member of the American Society of Home Inspectors, which has very strict membership requirements. You can log on to their web site to find members who are located in your area at www.ashi.org/find.

How to Conduct a Property Inspection

Unlike most real estate investors, I am a journeyman carpenter, with over 30 years of hands-on experience inspecting various types of residential and commercial properties. So, when I conduct an inspection, I show up at the property in my old coveralls with my clipboard and inspection checklists, searchlight, high-powered binoculars, mini-tape recorder, digital camera, and ice pick. I use the binoculars to inspect the roof, chimney, fascia, and soffit. The ice pick is used to check wood for dry rot and termite damage. I use the mini-tape recorder to record detailed descriptions of needed repairs. And the digital camera is used to take pictures of needed repairs, which are e-mailed to contractors to obtain repair cost estimates. The main thing that I am looking out for during my inspections is any type of structural damage that would be costly and time consuming to repair. For example, I recently inspected a run-down concrete block building, which had a leaky flat roof. During the inspection, I found four roof trusses located right smack-dab in the middle of the roof that were rotted beyond repair and needed replacement. I took pictures of the damaged area and e-mailed them to three Florida licensed building contractors and received repair cost estimates ranging from $12,000 to $18,000. I turned around and bought a one-year option on the property for $4,000 at a fixed purchase price, which was $20,000 below what I would have offered if I had not inspected the property and found the structural defect in the roof. In addition to inspecting the property itself, I always check out the neighborhood where the property is located between the hours of 8 P.M. and 12 P.M. During my neighborhood inspections, I check for excessive noise, cars parked in the street, rowdy parties with drunks wandering around, gang activity, and any other public nuisance that could adversely affect the property's resale value. I do this to avoid buying properties in neighborhoods that are placid during the day but become ugly after dark. I drive through neighborhoods after a heavy rainfall to check for drainage and flooding problems.

Be on the Lookout for Indoor Mold When Inspecting Properties

Today, the public perception surrounding indoor mold is such that even the suspicion that a building has just a smidgen of indoor mold is enough to strike fear into the hearts of most prospective buyers and stop them from pursuing the property. The fact of the matter is that probably every residential property in the United States contains a small amount of indoor mold, especially in bathrooms. I have no qualms whatsoever about buying a property with moderate amounts of indoor mold. And I have bought options on properties in which all of the walls and ceilings in both bathrooms were black with indoor mold. I had the moldy drywall replaced by a professional and turned around and sold my options. I am not afraid of properties with moderate amounts of indoor mold because I understand what causes it to grow and how to quickly clean it up. I know that mold thrives indoors where there is moisture, still air, and darkness, and that the following three conditions must be present in order for indoor mold to grow:

1. A source of nutrients such as wood, drywall, carpeting, floor and ceiling tiles.
2. Any source of moisture.
3. An optimum temperature with high humidity.

Indoor Mold Information Available Online

The following web sites have information on indoor mold:

EPA Mold Resources: www.epa.gov/iaq/pubs/moldresources.html

EPA Sick Building Syndrome: www.epa.gov/iaq/pubs/sbs.html

Mold and Fungi Assessment and Remediation: www.nyc.gov/html/doh /html/epi/moldrpt1.html

EPA Guide on How to Prevent and Clean Up Indoor Mold Growth

The EPA has published an excellent guide on how to prevent and clean up indoor mold growth, *A Brief Guide to Mold, Moisture, and Your Home,* which is available online at the following web page: www.epa.gov/iaq/molds/moldguide.html.

How to Inspect Suspicious Properties for Environmental Contamination

To avoid buying a potential toxic waste dump, have suspicious properties inspected for various types of environmental contamination that could make a property uninhabitable and render it worthless. A *suspicious property* is a property that has been used to house businesses such as gas stations, dry cleaners, automobile repair shops, and other businesses that use petroleum products, cleaning solvents, and hazardous chemicals. Even if you do not suspect that a property has any type of environmental contamination, use the following Phase One Environmental Audit Checklist to conduct your own inspection.

Sample Phase One Environmental Audit Checklist

1. Examine the property's chain of ownership for the past 50 years.
2. Interview the current and available past owners of the property to determine if any present or past uses of the property would have an adverse effect on the environment.
3. Review available past city cross-reference street directories to determine how the property was previously used.
4. Review available topographic maps of the property.
5. Review available historical aerial photographs of the property.
6. Review available geological reports affecting the property.
7. Research local, state, and federal government files for records of environmental problems affecting the property.
8. Research local, state, and federal government files for records of environmental problems affecting adjacent properties.
9. Conduct an onsite inspection of the property for obvious signs of past or present environmental problems such as odors, soil staining, stress vegetation, or evidence of dumping or burial.
10. Determine the existence and condition of above-ground storage tanks.
11. Determine the existence and condition of underground storage tanks.

Environmental Hazardous Waste Search Online

To perform an online environmental hazardous waste search on a property, log on to the following web sites:

EPA superfund hazardous waste site search: www.epa.gov/superfund/sites/query/basic.htm

Environmental hazards zip code search: www.scorecard.org

EPA Enviromapper zip code search: www.epa.gov/cgi-bin/enviro/empact/getZipCode.cgi?appl=empact&info=zipcode

HUD environmental maps: www.hud.gov/offices/cio/emaps/index.cfm

Housing Built Before 1978 May Pose Potential Lead-Based Paint Hazards

The Residential Lead-Based Paint Hazard Reduction Act requires that all sale agreements to sell residential property built before 1978 contain a Seller's Lead-Based Paint Disclosure Statement that discloses whether the property has been inspected for lead-based paint hazards and whether lead-based paint hazards have been found on the property.

Lead-Based Paint Hazard Information Online

The following is a listing of online sources of lead-based paint hazard information:

> EPA National Lead Information Center: www.epa.gov/lead/nlic.htm
>
> Lead-Based Paint Disclosure Fact Sheet: www.epa.gov/opptintr/lead /fs-discl.pdf
>
> Lessor's Lead-Based Paint Disclosure Statement: www.epa.gov/opptintr/lead /lesr_eng.pdf
>
> HUD Lead-Based Paint Abatement Guidelines: www.lead-info.com /abatementguidelinesexamp.html
>
> EPA Lead information pamphlet: www.hud.gov/lea/leapame.pdf

Use My Inspection Checklists to Conduct Your Pre-Buy Property Inspections

Last, the following pages contain my pre-buy property inspection checklists. My inspection checklists are unique because they all contain a repair cost column to allow the inspector to use the same form to do a rough repair cost estimate. My downloadable inspection forms allow for a fast, but thorough, inspection of any property.

_____
FORM 11.1   Sample Exterior Property Checklist
_____

Street address _____

Item	Good	Fair	Bad	Repair Cost
Roof				
Foundation				
Siding				
Windows				
Doors				
Carport				
Garage				
Paint				
Screens				
Soffit and fascia				
Chimney				
Steps				
Other				

FORM 11.2   Sample Grounds Inspection Checklist

Street address _____

Item	Good	Fair	Bad	Repair Cost
Lawn				
Plants and shrubs				
Trees				
Driveway				
Sidewalks				
Pot holes				
Sink holes				
Drainage				
Streets				
Outside lighting				
Other				

FORM 11.3   Sample Attic Inspection Checklist

Street address _____

Item	Good	Fair	Bad	Repair Cost
Ventilation				
Insulation				
Floor				
Lighting				
Roof rafters				
Ceiling joists				
Wiring				
Air Ducts				
Termite damage				
Mold				
Other				

FORM 11.4   Sample Garage and Carport Inspection Checklist

Street address _____

Item	Good	Fair	Bad	Repair Cost
Walls				
Floor				
Ceiling				
Doors				
Windows				
Lighting				
Heat				
Air conditioning				
Paint				
Roof				
Soffit and fascia				
Mold				
Other				

FORM 11.5   Sample Electrical Inspection Checklist

Street address _____

Item	Good	Fair	Bad	Repair Cost
Riser				
Service panel				
Capacity				
Circuit breakers				
Electrical outlets				
Lighting				
Wiring				
Electrical meter				
Other				

FORM 11.6   Sample Plumbing Inspection Checklist

Street address _____

Item	Good	Fair	Bad	Repair Cost
Water supply				
Hot water heater				
Toilets				
Sinks				
Tub				
Shower				
Septic system				
Water pipes				
Drains and sewer lines				
Water pressure				
Plumbing fixtures				
Water supply lines				
Well				
Mold				
Other				

FORM 11.7   Sample Heating and Air Conditioning Inspection Checklist

Street address _____

Item	Good	Fair	Bad	Repair Cost
Natural gas				
Central heat and air				
Oil furnace				
Window and wall units				
Solar panels				
Vents				
Condenser unit				
Heat pump				
Mold				
Other				

FORM 11.8   Sample Kitchen Inspection Checklist

Street address _____

Item	Good	Fair	Bad	Repair Cost
Floor				
Walls				
Ceiling				
Doors				
Windows				
Lighting				
Electrical outlets				
Sink				
Plumbing				
Cabinets				
Countertops				
Refrigerator				
Oven				
Ceramic tile				
Paint				
Mold				
Other				

FORM 11.9   Sample Bathroom Inspection Checklist

Street address _____

Item	Good	Fair	Bad	Repair Cost
Floor				
Walls				
Ceiling				
Doors				
Windows				
Lighting				
Electrical outlets				
Shower				
Toilets				
Tub				
Ceramic tile				
Sink and vanity				
Ventilation				
Linen closet				
Mirrors				
Paint				
Mold				
Other				

FORM 11.10   Sample Dining Room Inspection Checklist

Street address _____

Item	Good	Fair	Bad	Repair Cost
Floor				
Walls				
Ceiling				
Doors				
Windows				
Lighting				
Electrical outlets				
Paint				
Carpet				
Mold				
Other				

FORM 11.11   Sample Living Room Inspection Checklist

Street address _____

Item	Good	Fair	Bad	Repair Cost
Floor				
Walls				
Ceiling				
Doors				
Windows				
Lighting				
Electrical outlets				
Paint				
Carpet				
Mold				
Other				

FORM 11.12   Sample Bedroom Inspection Checklist

Street address _____

Item	Good	Fair	Bad	Repair Cost
Floor				
Walls				
Ceiling				
Windows				
Doors				
Lighting				
Electrical outlets				
Closets				
Carpet				
Paint				
Mold				
Other				

FORM 11.13   Sample Home Office Inspection Checklist

Street address _____

Item	Good	Fair	Bad	Repair Cost
Floor				
Walls				
Ceiling				
Windows				
Doors				
Lighting				
Electrical outlets				
Storage closets				
Carpet				
Paint				
Mold				
Other				

CHAPTER 12

How to Accurately Estimate a Property's Current Market Value

From what I have seen over the years, buying options on overpriced properties is the number one reason many people fail to make it in the real estate option investment business. And for most beginning option investors, overestimating the value of their first option property usually proves to be a very costly and often a fatal mistake, which generally marks the beginning of the end of their foray of investing in real estate options. You must understand that when you assign or sell a real estate option to a third party, what you are really selling is the property under option. This means that if the property under option has a purchase price that is right at or above market value, it will be nearly impossible to find anyone willing to buy your real estate option. I know an investor in Las Vegas, Nevada, who learned this lesson the hard way when he bought a one-year option for $10,000 on a former gas station, which had been sitting vacant for two years. This neophyte investor overestimated the property's current market value by $40,000. The way that this guy explained his big-time blunder to me in an e-mail message was that he never bothered to verify the owner's claim that the underground tanks were in tip-top shape and that everything was just hunky-dory. This very naïve rookie had bought the option under the wrongful assumption that he could just turn around and resell the property as a ready-to-go gas station. This guy got a real wakeup call when a prospective buyer's preliminary due diligence turned up a Nevada Department of Environmental Protection leaking tank list with the property on it. According to this guy's e-mail, the investor who found out about the leaky storage tanks waited until his option expired and bought the property from the unscrupulous owner for $60,000 below his purchase price.

Definition of Current Market Value

For the purpose of this book, I define the term *current market value* as the value of a property after deducting all of the costs associated with getting the property into a marketable resale condition. To illustrate, a couple of years ago, I bought a one-year option for $3,500 on a vacant, run-down single-family house, which was located in an emerging commercial area of Brandon, Florida, a suburb of Tampa. The out-of-town owner initially asked $85,000 for the property. I calculated the property's current market value to be right around $55,000 after deducting $30,000 in needed repairs and upgrades. And that is what I offered her for it. She made a counteroffer of $65,000, which I accepted. I turned around and had the property rezoned for use as a professional office and sold my option six months later for $25,000. But I would have never been able to realize a $21,000 profit on the deal if I had paid her initial asking price of $85,000 instead of $65,000, which was closer to my estimated current market value of $55,000.

The Definition of Market Value

The Appraisal Foundation's Uniform Standards of Professional Appraisal Practice defines *market value* as: "the most probable price a property should bring in a competitive and open market under all conditions requisite to a fair sale, the buyer and seller each acting prudently and knowledgeably, and assuming the sale price isn't affected by undue stimulus." This definition assumes that the following conditions are met:

1. The buyer and seller are motivated.
2. Each party is well informed and acting in his or her own best interests.
3. A reasonable amount of time is allowed for the property to be exposed on the open market.
4. Payment is made in cash in U.S. dollars or in comparable financial arrangements.
5. The price represents the normal consideration of the property sold and is unaffected by special or creative financing or sales concessions granted by anyone associated with the sale.

The Difference between Assessed Value and Appraised Value

The difference between a property's tax-assessed value and its appraised value is as follows:

1. *Tax-assessed value* is the value established by the local taxing authority for a parcel of land and the improvements placed upon the land for property tax purposes. For example, in Florida, owner-occupied single-family houses are generally assessed at around 70 percent of their fair market value by county property appraisers.

2. *Appraised value* is the value estimate given to a property by a licensed property appraiser using accepted appraisal methods for the type of property being appraised. For example, the accepted appraisal method to accurately estimate the fair market value for an owner-occupied single-family house is the comparison sales method where a property's value is based on the recent sale of comparable properties within the same area.

The Definition of a Property Appraisal Report

A *property appraisal report* prepared by a licensed property appraiser is generally defined as: "an opinion or estimate of a property's value based on a thorough analysis of all the available data that's been derived from one or all three of the property appraisal valuation methods that are commonly used to appraise property."

To avoid being snookered by dishonest property owners who use bogus appraisal reports to help substantiate the asking price for their property, you must know what to look for when reading a residential or commercial property appraisal report. A sham appraisal report is not that difficult to spot when you know what to look for. The best way to check the validity of an appraisal report is to use an appraisal report checklist, such as the sample on page 134.

The Three Common Methods Used by Appraisers to Estimate Property Values

The three common methods used by property appraisers to estimate property values are the:

1. *Comparison sales method:* The comparison sales method bases a property's value on the recent sale prices of properties within the same area and comparable in size, quality, amenities, and features.

2. *Income method:* The income method is used to estimate the value of an income-producing property based on the net income the property produces.

3. *Replacement cost method:* The replacement cost method is based on what it would cost to replace the improvements on property using similar construction materials and construction methods.

FORM 12.1   Sample Property Appraisal Report Checklist

1. Is the purpose for the appraisal accurately stated in the appraisal?

2. Is there a certificate of value included with the appraisal?

3. Does the appraisal include a summary of conclusions?

4. Does the appraisal analysis identify significant trends?

5. Does the appraisal focus on the factors affecting the property's value?

6. Does the appraisal describe the economic base?

7. Does the appraisal describe the property's neighborhood?

8. Does the appraisal describe neighborhood trends?

9. Does the appraisal contain errors in mathematical computations?

10. Does the appraisal contain errors in land, area and building sizes?

11. Does the appraisal include an adequate history of the property?

12. Do the photographs contained in the appraisal adequately show the property?

13. Is the appraisal written in a clear, concise, complete, consistent and factual manner?

14. Does the appraisal outline both the negative and positive features of the property?

15. Does the appraisal contain inconsistencies between the market comparison, income and replacement cost methods, remaining economic life and depreciation?

16. Were recent comparable sales used in the appraisal?

17. Was special financing used in any comparable sales?

18. Were more than three comparable sales used in the appraisal?

19. Were comparable property sale locations similar to the subject property being appraised?

20. Were all comparable sales data fully analyzed and adjusted?

21. Is the subject property compatible with other properties in the area?

22. Are comparable sales locations being put to their best use?

23. Was the market data used to calculate the capitalization rate selected from similar properties within the same market area?

24. Were vacancy and rent collection losses and operating expenses included in calculating the capitalization rate?

25. Does the current market data support the capitalization rate?

The Comparison Sales Method of Estimating a Property's Value

The comparison sales method of estimating a property's value is based on the recent sale prices of properties within the same area that are comparable in size, amenities, and features. In order to be accurate, sale price adjustments must be made for comparable properties that have been sold at unrealistically low prices or on overly favorable financial terms, not readily available to the buying public.

Online Sources of Comparable Residential Property Sales

Comparable sales data for residential property are available online at the following web sites:

DataQuick: www.dataquick.com

HomeGain: www.homegain.com

REAL-COMP: www.real-comp.com

HomeRadar: www.homeradar.com

Domania Home Price Check: www.domania.com

Online Sources of Comparable Commercial Property Sale and Income Data

Comparable sale and income data for all types of commercial properties are readily available online for free or for a relatively small fee at the following web sites:

CoStar Exchange: www.costar.com

Loopnet: www.loopnet.com

National Real Estate Index: www.realestateindex.com

IDM Corporation: www.idmdata-now.com

DataQuick: www.dataquick.com

Apartment Comparable Sales: www.apartmentcomps.com

Real Estate Information Source: www.reis.com

The Income Method of Estimating a Property's Value

The income method is used to estimate the value of an income-producing property, based on the net income the property produces. Under the income method, value is calculated using a:

1. *Capitalization rate:* The capitalization rate, or cap rate, is calculated by dividing a property's annual net operating income by its purchase price.
2. *Gross rent multiplier:* The gross rent multiplier (GRM) is calculated by dividing the purchase price by the property's monthly gross operating income.

How to Calculate a Property's Capitalization Rate

To calculate the capitalization rate or cap rate, you would divide the property's annual net operating income by its estimated value. For example, a property with an annual net operating income of $36,000 and an estimated value of $360,000 would have a cap rate of 10 percent ($36,000 ÷ $360,000 = 10). In most markets, cap rates between 9 percent and 11 percent are considered good. In most markets, it is hard to find reliable capitalization rate data for small commercial properties. That's because in most markets, there are generally fewer sales of small commercial properties from which to gather comparable property sales and income data. This results in property appraisers having to construct capitalization rates that are not based on verifiable sales and income data, but rather on what is known in certain property appraisal circles as the SWAG Principle, which is an acronym for "some wild ass guess." Unless you can find bona fide cap rate data that is based on actual sales of comparable small commercial properties, I would be leery of using any cap rates that were nothing more than a figment of some owner's or appraiser's imagination. The point that I am making here is that you do not want to estimate a property's current market value based on a bogus capitalization rate. Depending on the volume of sales in your market, you should be able to get capitalization rate data from local:

1. Property appraiser's or assessor's office.
2. Apartment owners' association.
3. Commercial mortgage lenders.
4. Commercial property appraisers.

How to Use Gross Rent Multipliers to Estimate an Income Property's Value

To calculate the GRM, divide the estimated value of the property by its annual effective gross rental income. I prefer using an annual GRM instead of the monthly version. Effective gross rental income refers to the actual rental income that was collected with the vacancy and credit loss factored in, and not the potential gross income. For example, a small, six-unit rental property with an estimated value of $250,000 and a gross annual rental income of $36,000 would have an annual GRM of 7 when rounded up to the next whole number ($250,000 ÷ $36,000 = 6.94). In most markets, investors need a GRM between 7 and 10 to earn a reasonable profit.

Watch Out for Owners Using Fuzzy Math on Income and Expense Statements

To be successful in this business, you must be willing to delve beyond the numbers that are posted on monthly income and expense statements when estimating the current market value of rental properties. A word to the wise: When you read a property's income and expense statement, you should always go under the assumption that the owner is probably practicing fuzzy math by fudging on the numbers and telling little white lies to back them up. And I am not the least bit bashful about asking property owners to provide me with verifiable documentation to support the numbers they are claiming on their income and expense statements. Also, do not fall victim to pie-in-the-sky income projections, which overly optimistic property owners often try to foist upon gullible investors. As far as I am concerned, if owners cannot or will not provide verifiable documentation to support their income and expenses, I dismiss the whole kit and caboodle as being 100 percent unadulterated bullspit. In other words, when you come across property owners whom you suspect of practicing their own version of Creative Accounting 101, you should pretty much discount most of what they are claiming on their books as income and expenses. In addition, watch out for property owners using rent concessions, such as a free month's rent to help fill vacancies prior to putting their property up for sale. What generally happens is that the last month in the tenancy, usually after the property has been sold, the free month's rent kicks in. The best defense against being victimized by property owners who cook their books is to take a see-it-to-believe-it attitude and reconcile everything that is listed on a property's monthly income and expense statement against what is shown on:

1. Schedule E, Supplemental Income and Loss, of the owner's latest federal income tax return.
2. The property's latest annual tax assessment income and expense statement on file at the county property appraiser or assessor's office.
3. All of the rental agreements for the past year.
4. Water, sewage, solid waste, gas, and electric bills and receipts for the past year.
5. Repair and capital improvement bills and receipts for the past year.

Require Owners to Provide Verifiable Documentation to Support Their Tax Returns

Do not allow yourself to be bamboozled by unscrupulous property owners using bogus federal income tax returns to back up their creative bookkeeping. Insist that all annual income and expense statements be supported by federal tax returns. You need to have this information so that you can verify that what you are being told jibes with what owners are claiming on their federal income tax returns. And the only way to do this is ask property owners to complete and sign IRS Form 4506, Request for Copy or Transcript of Tax Form, so that you can order a copy of the owner's Schedule E that has been filed with the IRS. However, I have found that in most cases, owners will refuse your request on the grounds that what is on their federal income tax return "is none of your damn business." When this happens to you, do what I do: Make a really lowball offer on the property, and if it is not accepted, move on to the next deal.

Reconcile the Rent Roll against the Rental Rates Listed in Rental Agreements

To avoid being swindled by lying owners who overstate their property's rental income, you must always reconcile the rental rates listed on the rent roll against the rental rates stated in the rental agreements. For example, I once had an owner who claimed on the rent roll that the gross rental income for a six-unit rental property during the past year was $39,600 (6 units × $550 × 12 months) when the contract rental rates listed in the rental agreements showed that only four units were rented for $550 a month while the other two were rented for $500. Use the income and expense analysis worksheet on page 139 for your reconciliation.

FORM 12.2   Sample Monthly Income and Expense Analysis Worksheet

1. Gross monthly rental income: $_____

2. Total monthly income: $_____

3. Less vacancy allowance and credit losses: $_____

4. Gross monthly operating income: $_____

5. Property taxes (divide annual amount by 12): $_____

6. License fees (divide annual amount by 12): $_____

7. Property management fee: $_____

8. Employee wages and benefits: $_____

9. Natural gas: $_____

10. Electricity: $_____

11. Trash removal: $_____

12. Water and sewer: $_____

13. Telephone: $_____

14. Internet: $_____

15. Advertising: $_____

16. Building maintenance and repairs: $_____

17. Lawn care and landscaping: $_____

18. Swimming pool maintenance and repair: $_____

19. Parking, walkway and driveway maintenance: $_____

20. Insurance premiums (divide annual amount by 12): $_____

21. Maintenance and office supplies: $_____

22. Automobile expenses: $_____

23. Net monthly operating income: $_____

The Replacement Cost Method of Estimating a Property's Value

The replacement cost method of estimating a property's value is based on the cost of replacing the improvements on the property minus the cost of the land to estimate a property's value. Replacement costs are calculated on a per square foot basis by dividing the total number of square feet in the building by the per square foot construction cost. For example, a 2000 square foot convenience store that cost $275,000 to build would have a replacement cost of $137.50 per square foot ($275,000 ÷ 2000). You can usually get a free building replacement cost estimate by calling a local independent insurance broker who represents insurers that specialize in providing property and casualty insurance coverage for residential and commercial buildings. Property replacement costs are calculated by using a replacement cost formula that is based on the property's geographical location and its:

1. Street address.
2. Age.
3. Type of construction.
4. Number of stories.
5. Type of roof.
6. Current use.
7. Heating and cooling system.
8. Square footage.

Deduct the Total Fix-Up Cost When Calculating the Property's Current Value

To get an accurate estimate of a potential option property's current market value, you must deduct the total cost necessary to fix up the property in order to maximize its curb appeal and resale value. The best way to do this is to use the information that you gathered about the property's physical condition during your property inspection and complete a property fix-up cost estimate worksheet like the sample on page 141 to calculate the property's total fix-up cost.

Always Verify Loan Information Directly with Lenders

To calculate how much equity an owner has in a property, you must first know the unpaid principal loan balance. However, the only way to verify the balance

FORM 12.3   Sample Property Fix-Up Cost Estimate Worksheet

Repair Item	Estimated Cost
Soffit, fascia, gutters and downspouts	$_____
Roofs, flashing and vents	$_____
Lawn, shrubs and plants	$_____
Parking areas and walkways	$_____
Fences and walls	$_____
Exterior door repair and replacement	$_____
Exterior building repair, preparation and paint	$_____
Exterior lighting repair and replacement	$_____
Countertop repair and replacement	$_____
Plumbing repair and replacement	$_____
Window repair and replacement	$_____
Carpet cleaning and replacement	$_____
Cabinet repair and replacement	$_____
Interior preparation and paint	$_____
Interior door repair and replacement	$_____
Electrical repair and replacement	$_____
Vinyl and ceramic tile replacement	$_____
Heating and cooling system repair and replacement	$_____
Other	$_____

Total cost estimate $_____

and the payment status of a mortgage or deed of trust loan is for the lender to provide the owner with an estoppel letter, which states the unpaid loan balance and the payment status of the loan. Estoppel is a legal doctrine that prevents parties from denying facts that they have previously certified as being true. For example, if a lender sends you an estoppel letter stating that Mr. and Mrs. John Q. Public's mortgage or deed of trust loan has an outstanding balance of $52,750 as of a specific date, the lender cannot later claim that the loan balance was really $62,750. I recommend that you have the property owner call the lender to get the name of the person in charge of the loan servicing customer service department before sending the estoppel letter. This way, the owner will have the name of a real live person to call if he or she does not receive a quick response to the estoppel letter request. To request a mortgage or deed of trust estoppel letter from a lender, send a letter like the sample on page 143.

Use My Eight-Step Approach to Estimating a Property's Current Market Value

I recommend that you use my eight-step approach to estimate a potential option property's current market value:

Step 1: Log on to your county's property appraiser or assessor's web site to obtain the tax-assessed value of the property under consideration for purchase.

Step 2: Search your county's property tax rolls for recent sales of three to five properties that are comparable in size, amenities, and features and located within one mile of the property under consideration for purchase.

Step 3: Carefully analyze any comparable properties that you find, and make sale price adjustments for differences in amenities, special features, and the property's physical condition.

Step 4: Verify the income and expenses, which are listed on the income and expense statement of the property under consideration.

Step 5: Analyze the property's income and expenses for the past 12 months to estimate its net operating income potential.

Step 6: Calculate the property's capitalization rate by dividing its potential operating income by the estimated value, which you derived from analyzing recent sales of comparable properties in Step 3.

Step 7: Estimate the property's value by multiplying its net operating income by the capitalization rate that you came up with for the property.

FORM 12.4   Sample Estoppel Letter to Lenders

May 24, 2005

Ms. Karen Burns
Manager
Bank of South Florida
6970 Fowler Avenue
Tampa, FL 33647

Reference mortgage loan number: SFL082819501
Mortgagor: Robert J. Johnson

Dear Ms. Burns:

Please send a facsimile of the following information regarding my mortgage loan to Mr. David D. Jones at (555) 123-4567 or via e-mail to ddjones@hotmail.com.

Principal and interest payment $_____   Original loan amount $_____

Insurance payment $_____   Date of original loan _____

Tax payment $_____   Payment due date _____

Interest rate _____   Escrow impound balance $_____

Total monthly payment $_____   Principal balance $_____

Current status of the loan $_____

Thank you for your prompt attention to this matter.

Sincerely,

Robert J. Johnson

FORM 12.5   Sample Current Market Value Worksheet

1. Tax assessed value: $_____

2. Appraised value: $_____

3. Type of property: $_____

4. Type of construction: $_____

5. Year built: $_____

6. Type of units: $_____

7. Number of units: $_____

8. First mortgage or deed of trust loan balance: $_____

9. Second mortgage or deed of trust loan balance: $_____

10. Amount of all liens and judgments recorded against the property: $_____

11. Amount of annual property taxes: $_____

12. Amount of all outstanding city, county, and state fines: $_____

13. Total amount owed against the property: $_____

14. Property's estimated fix-up costs: $_____

15. Property's estimated current market value: $_____

16. Property's estimated replacement cost: $_____

17. Owner's estimated equity: $_____

Step 8: Calculate the cost of replacing the improvements on the property by using the same building materials and method of construction.

Use the current market value worksheet above as a guide when calculating a property's market value.

CHAPTER 13

How to Negotiate Low-Cost Options and Below-Market Purchase Prices with Property Owners

In my more than 24 years as a real estate investor, I have seen real estate investors ranging from neophytes just starting out to self-proclaimed seasoned veterans get snookered into overpaying for property, all because they were unable, for whatever reason, to master the fundamentals of negotiations. This hapless group of investors failed to grasp the very basic concept that when it comes to the terms of a real estate transaction, everything, and I do mean everything, is negotiable. They did not understand that, unlike your local Home Depot where every item in the store's inventory has a universal product code or UPC that lists the product's non-negotiable sale price, how much you pay for a real estate option or property really depends on how good a negotiator you are. And if you are a shrewd negotiator, you can buy low-cost real estate options and properties at below-market purchase prices. But, if you are a poor negotiator, you will probably end up paying way too much for your first and, most likely, your last real estate option. In this business, when you start off by overpaying for a real estate option or property, you put yourself behind a sort of financial eight ball, which can be very hard to get out from behind unless you are extremely lucky and can resell the option or property to an uninformed investor who is willing to pay more than what it is worth. However, if you cannot find an unwitting adherent to the greater fool theory, your costly mistake will come right off the top of your resale profit, which may result in a breakeven deal at best. And I have yet to meet anyone who has become a profitable real estate option investor by doing breakeven deals!

Most Americans Don't Like to Negotiate

I had the opportunity to hone my negotiating skills while haggling with store-owners in Seoul, South Korea, and with flea market vendors throughout Western Europe. And unlike the vast majority of my fellow Americans, I very quickly learned how to master the negotiating game in both places. I was able to do this because I always took the attitude of: "When in Rome, do as the Romans," and observed how the locals conducted business. I ended up running a thriving antique wall and mantle clock business. I bought old clocks—the real estate equivalent of fixer-uppers—at flea markets in Germany, Holland, Belgium, France, Italy, and Luxembourg and had them cleaned up and repaired. I then resold them to my fellow Americans for a substantial profit because they were afraid to venture out onto the local economy. As a result of my observations, both here and abroad, I have come to the conclusion that most people in the good old U.S.A. would rather have a root canal performed on them than try to negotiate any type of purchase price with a seller. Perhaps this is because most Americans view negotiating more as a full contact sport than as an opportunity to better their position in a real estate transaction. The fact is, as a nation, we are not very good hagglers. Most Americans will spend more time and energy dickering over a $200 item with an automobile salesperson than they ever will over the price of a piece of property worth hundreds of thousands of dollars. America may come across to many in the outside world as a nation of overly aggressive hucksters, but deep down, Mr. and Mrs. America would rather pay full retail than cause a ruckus by making a big deal over the price! If you want to get a first-hand look at how not to conduct any type of negotiations, just hang around a car dealership or real estate brokerage office on a Saturday afternoon and observe the one-sided negotiations that take place between the sales staff and their customers!

Some Property Owners View Negotiations as a Sort of Cat and Mouse Game

For whatever reason, some property owners are overly coy about clearly stating the asking price for their property. When questioned about their asking price, they mumble something to the effect of, "Make me an offer." This type of owner seems to view selling property as a sort of cat and mouse game, in which the owner assumes the role of the cat, while assigning prospective buyers the role of mice. I do not know about you, but I am not too keen on playing cat and mouse games with anyone, especially not with property owners who are not serious sellers. When you meet owners like this, do as I do and nonchalantly hand them one of your business cards and ask them to please call when they decide on an asking price. Doing this will usually cause the property owner to mutter something along the lines of: "Well, aren't you even going to make me an offer before you leave?" At this point, I politely inform the owner that I am running late for my next appointment to look at another property. If you handle this type of scenario in the detached, professional manner that I have just described, more times than not, the property owner will contact you later on to see if you are still interested in buying an option on the property. At this point, the owner has outsmarted himself or herself and unwittingly put you in a position of power, from which you should be able to negotiate a low-cost real estate option and below-market purchase price on buyer-friendly terms.

Many Property Owners Are Fervent Believers in the Greater Fool Theory

As you will soon find out, many property owners are fervent believers in what is rightfully called the *greater fool theory*. The greater fool theory is based on the inane assumption that so-called investors who make bad buying decisions will eventually be able to pass their blunders on to bigger or greater fools who will unknowingly buy them out at an equal or greater price than what they paid. And believe me, owners with this mindset have an extremely hard time accepting reality-based logic. The greater fool theory is exactly why, initially, many property owners have unrealistic expectations when it comes to what their property is really worth in its current condition. They fail to grasp why people like me are not willing to bail them out of their financial fiasco and simply pay them what they overpaid for their property. So, during the early stages of negotiations, the favorite expression of most reality-challenged property owners is: "Surely you do not expect me to sell you my property for less than what I paid for it?" My retort to this response is always the same: "If I do make you an offer, it will be based strictly on what I estimate the property to be worth today in its current condition, and not on what you paid for it!" I say this so that owners know right from the get-go that I am not going to play the role of the greater fool and subsidize their adventures as real estate investors. At this point, owners either become realistic and negotiations continue, or they hold out for their greater fool in shining armor, and I give them my business card and move on to the next potential option property.

Always Verify the Identity of the Property Owner before You Begin Negotiations

First things first: To avoid being flimflammed by an identity thief posing as the property owner of record, make certain that the person you are negotiating with is the owner and not an imposter. The best way to verify that the person you are meeting with is, in fact, the property owner is to do what I do when I meet with an owner for the first time: Show your driver's license, and ask the owner to do likewise. As I show the owner my Florida driver's license, I matter-of-factly explain that I am doing this because of the rampant spread of identity theft. And if for whatever reason, the owner refuses to identify who he or she is by showing me some form of government-issued photo identification, I politely excuse myself and get up and leave. So far, I have met with only one property owner who refused to show me a photo identification.

Six Basic Rules to Follow When Negotiating with Property Owners

I suggest that you follow my six basic rules when negotiating real estate option and purchase agreements with property owners:

Rule 1: As the old saying goes, first impressions are lasting impressions, and this is especially true when you begin negotiating with property owners. The image that you want to project is that of a savvy, polished professional investor. Please understand that when I use the term *polished professional*, I am not referring to the slick-looking bozos and bimbos who make their living by starring in infomercials on television. Polished professionals are individuals who are sincere, personable, confident, knowledgeable, well spoken, well mannered, well groomed, and in control of their emotions and not like the typical real estate investor who often comes across as a confused, uninformed, clueless flake, looking like he or she just came from a Grateful Dead concert. The point I am making here is that if you want to be taken seriously by property owners, you must act like a responsible adult who is ready, willing, and able to negotiate.

Rule 2: As a negotiator, do not try to be what you are not. If you consider yourself to be a mild-mannered, soft-spoken type of person, do not try to assume the role of a pushy loudmouth just for the sake of negotiations. Instead, adopt a negotiating style that is more in line with your personality. This way, you can be a successful negotiator without having to change your natural personality. For the record, most mild-mannered, soft-spoken people usually make the best negotiators because they are generally nonconfrontational, and most people underestimate them at the bargaining table. But regardless of the type of personality that you possess, if you want to become an excellent negotiator, you must first become an excellent listener. Never forget that the reason we human beings have two ears and one mouth is the better to hear with. Please keep this in mind the next time you get the urge to speak out of turn while the other party is still talking.

Rule 3: Limit the use of tall tales, little white lies, and fibs to describing fishing and hunting exploits and not your background. The fastest way to lose credibility during negotiations is to get caught in a boldfaced lie. I immediately cease negotiating with anyone who tries the old dazzle them with brilliance and baffle them with bullspit technique on me. I do this because I have adopted a zero tolerance policy, which prevents me from negotiating with people who employ games, gimmicks, and bullspit as a major part of their negotiating strategy. Years ago I made a solemn vow to myself that I would never again waste my valuable time and energy negotiating with ethically challenged people who cannot make the distinction between fact and fiction.

Rule 4: When negotiating with property owners, use the time-tested KISS principle: Keep it simple, stupid. In other words, do not go off on a long-winded, full-blown technical tangent when explaining to a property owner how a real estate option transaction works. The point here is to never forget that the object of your negotiations is to obtain low-cost real estate options and below-market purchase prices, not to impress property owners with your real estate expertise. Nothing more! Any unnecessary tricky stuff has the potential to confuse the property owner and kill the deal. Save the fancy words and technical terms for discussions with your board-certified real estate attorney, the title or escrow agent handling the transaction, and your fellow real estate option investors!

Rule 5: Never negotiate with people who do not have the authority to say yes. In other words, do not waste your valuable time trying to negotiate a real estate option agreement through a third party, such as an attorney, accountant, or real estate broker, who is acting only as an intermediary. Instead, find out right upfront before negotiations begin whether the person that you are dealing with has the authority to make a final decision and say yes. This is especially true when dealing with married couples and people with so-called partners. If the person that you begin negotiations with claims to have a spouse or partner, tell him or her that the only way that you will continue negotiations is if you can sit down face-to-face with both of them. The last thing that you want to happen during negotiations is to be involved in a situation where the person you are dealing with has to go to a higher authority for approval.

Rule 6: During every negotiating session, there comes a point when it is time to stop talking. But it is usually right at this very crucial point that most amateurs talk themselves right out of a deal because they simply do not know when to shut up. The time to stop talking is immediately after both you and the seller have had your say. This is the time to put up or shut up! In other words, it is time to either close on the purchase of a real estate option or agree to meet again after the owner has had time to mull things over, but it is not the time to ramble on.

Know What You Want before Negotiations Ever Begin

Never lose sight of that fact that your two main objectives when negotiating with property owners are to buy a real estate option at a price that is 5 percent or less of the property's current market value and to purchase the property at a price of at least 20 percent or more below its fair market value. And as a negotiator, I know what I want, and I know what I am willing to give to get it before negotiations ever begin. For example, before I ever sit down at the negotiating table, I already know:

1. The maximum amount I am willing to pay for a real estate option.
2. The maximum amount I am willing to pay for the property.
3. The terms of the real estate option agreement that I am willing to accept.
4. The terms of the purchase of the property that I am willing to accept.

Thirteen Crucial Terms That Must Be Negotiated in Every Option Agreement

Here are 13 crucial terms that must be negotiated in every real estate option agreement:

1. *Purchase price of the real estate option:* Negotiate a real estate option fee that does not exceed 5 percent of the property's current market value.
2. *Credit for cleaning up the property:* Obtain a $500 cleaning credit, to be applied toward the option fee, for cleaning up the property.
3. *Credit for the real estate option fee paid:* Require that the full amount of the option fee be credited toward the purchase price when the option is exercised.
4. *Length of the real estate option period:* Negotiate a 6- to 12-month option.
5. *Fixed purchase price of the property:* Negotiate the fixed purchase price of the property to include the amount of the down payment to be paid and how the purchase is to be financed.
6. *Right to extend the real estate option period:* Obtain the right to extend the option period for two 3- to 6-month periods, to include the cost of each extension period.

7. *Right to assign the real estate option agreement:* Negotiate the right to assign or sell the real estate option agreement to a third party during the option period.

8. *Option fee sole remedy for default:* Negotiate that the option fee paid is the sole and exclusive remedy in case you exercise the real estate option but fail to purchase the property.

9. *Refund of the option fee for eminent domain action:* Negotiate that the optionee will receive a full refund of the option fee plus any accrued interest if the property is condemned by eminent domain during the option period.

10. *Right to enter the property:* Obtain the right to enter, clean, market, repair, and show the property to prospective buyers during the option period.

11. *Right to a refund of the option fee for damage or destruction:* Obtain the right to a full refund of the option fee plus accrued interest if the property is severely damaged or destroyed by fire, storms, or earthquakes during the option period.

12. *Require title transfer documents be held in escrow:* Require that a warranty or grant deed and purchase agreement with the notarized signature of the optionor be held in escrow by a reputable attorney or title or escrow company during the option period.

13. *Right to record a memorandum of real estate option agreement:* Negotiate the right to record a memorandum of real estate option agreement in the official public records.

Five Negotiating Tools You Can Use to Obtain Lower Prices and Better Terms

If you followed my advice in Chapters 10 and 11 and thoroughly researched the property and its owner when performing due diligence and if you had the property thoroughly inspected, you should have a pretty good idea as to what information you can use to help negotiate favorable terms. Here are five negotiating tools that savvy real estate option investors can use to their advantage to negotiate low-cost real estate options and below-market purchase prices on buyer-friendly terms:

Negotiating Tool 1: The obsolescent flaws and physical condition of the property, based on property inspection reports, to include repair and cleanup cost estimates.

Negotiating Tool 2: The location of the property, to include the type and condition of adjacent properties.

Negotiating Tool 3: The financial condition of the individual or business entity that owns the property.

Negotiating Tool 4: Any stigmas attached to the property that affect the public's overall perception of the property.

Negotiating Tool 5: Any condemnation orders or accumulated fines for noncompliance with building, fire, safety, and health enforcement citations that affect the property's marketability.

Over the years, I have employed Negotiating Tool 5 to buy low-cost options on properties in Tampa that had been repeatedly cited for various code violations by the City of Tampa and were on the verge of being condemned for demolition. I focus on wooden, single-family houses that can be easily and inexpensively demolished, which are located on building lots with water and sewer hookups in place. But before I buy an option, I call the City of Tampa Code Enforcement Department and speak with the code inspector who is responsible for the area where the property is located to get the lowdown on the property. And if everything checks out okay, I go ahead and use the code enforcement action to negotiate a low-cost, 60-day option and below-market purchase price with the property owner. Once the property is under option, I market the property to all of the homebuilders in Tampa who specialize in building low-cost houses.

Use the Property's Physical and Financial Condition as Negotiating Tools

When negotiating the purchase price of a property, you must always use its physical and financial condition as tools to negotiate a below-market purchase price. To do this, use:

1. Inspection checklists.
2. Repair cost estimates.
3. Code violation citations.
4. Monthly income and expense statements.
5. Vacancy rate.
6. Operating expenses.

Negotiate a Cleaning Credit to Help Defray Your Property Cleanup Costs

Always try to negotiate a $500 cleaning credit to help defray your property cleanup costs. And have the $500 credit applied toward the option fee at the time the option agreement is signed and notarized. You will find that most owners of vacant, run-down properties will welcome your offer to clean up their property, especially if the property has been cited for violations by the local code enforcement department. Over the years, I have had only one property owner balk at giving me a $500 cleaning credit toward the option fee. And when it happened, I turned around and refused to sign the option agreement until the property was cleaned up.

Five FAQs Property Owners Often Pose When Negotiating Real Estate Options

In some cases, property owners will grill you about buying an option on their property. Here are the five most frequently asked questions that property owners pose when negotiating real estate option agreements, along with the suggested answers:

FAQ 1: What exactly is a real estate option?

Answer: It is a legal arrangement under which I pay you a non-refundable fee for the irrevocable right to purchase your property for a set price during a specific period of time.

FAQ 2: Why do you want to buy a real estate option instead of the property itself?

Answer: Because I am not ready to purchase the property right now, but I want to have the property available for when I am ready to buy it, and real estate options give me the flexibility to do this.

FAQ 3: Why should I agree to a fixed purchase price now instead of when the option is exercised?

Answer: Because I am agreeing to buy an option on your property in an as-is condition with no contingencies, and there is no incentive for me to buy options on properties that do not have a fixed purchase price at the time the real estate option agreement is signed.

FAQ 4: What happens if you do not exercise your option in time?

Answer: The option expires and you get to keep the entire option fee that I paid you.

FAQ 5: Why must I also sign a deed and purchase agreement at the same time we sign the real estate option agreement?

Answer: So that all of the documents that are needed to purchase the property will be readily available when the option is exercised.

Buy Real Estate Options at Prices 5 Percent or Less of the Property's Value

To gain maximum leverage when using real estate options and to avoid having all of your working capital tied up in real estate option fees, I recommend that you never pay more than 5 percent of a property's current market value for a real estate option. For example, on a property with a current market value of $250,000, you should never pay more than $12,500 for a one-year real estate option. In fact, I probably would not offer more than $10,000 for a one-year option on a property worth $250,000. And to reiterate what I told you at the beginning of this chapter, the amount that you wind up paying for a real estate option usually depends more on your skills as a negotiator than on the actual value of the property you are buying the option on. Depending on the condition of the property and the owner's circumstances, I usually start the price for a real estate option at $5,000 and increase it in $500 increments until I buy the option or cease negotiations.

Strive to Buy Properties at Prices 20 Percent or More below Market Value

For the purpose of this book, I define a *below-market* purchase price as a price that is at least 20 percent below the market value of a property in its current physical condition. And in order to have a reasonable expectation of earning a profit when using real estate options, you must buy options only on properties that can be bought at prices that are 20 percent or more below their current market value. For example, under my formula, you could not pay more than $230,000 for a property with a current market value of $287,500. Based on my experiences, 20 percent below market value is the bare minimum that will allow you to earn a reasonable return on the time, effort, and money involved in completing a real estate option transaction. Unless you want to work for below minimum wage, you had better walk away from any property that cannot be bought at a minimum of 20 percent below its current market value!

Why You Must Negotiate a Fixed Purchase Price at the Time You Buy the Option

Whatever you do when negotiating a real estate option, always insist that your real estate option agreement include a fixed purchase price for the property being put under option. And never agree to pay a purchase price based on the property's appraised value at the time the option is exercised. Doing so would defeat the whole purpose for using real estate options. After all, it would not make any sense financially to buy a real estate option without first locking in the purchase price of the property under option. As far as I am concerned, anyone who is foolish enough to buy a real estate option without knowing the actual purchase price of the property deserves to lose money! I once had a property owner, who I later found out was also a Florida licensed real estate broker, try to talk me into signing a one-year option agreement that included a clause stipulating that the purchase price of the property would be based on the property's tax-assessed value at the time the option was exercised, plus an additional $40,000. Needless to say, I told this guy what he could do with his cockamamie property valuation formula.

Determine How the Owner Came Up with the Asking Price for the Property

When an owner has an asking price for the property, find out how he or she came up with it. This question is critical because most owners are clueless when it comes to knowing how to accurately estimate their property's current market value. You will find that many owners oftentimes equate their property's value with what they paid for it, plus appreciation based on some convoluted mathematical formula that has nothing to do with reality. Once you get the answer to this question, you will pretty much know whether you are dealing with a reasonable, rational, intelligent, reality-based adult or a die-hard believer in the greater fool theory! Your next step is to show the property owner in a non-confrontational manner the verifiable sale and income data that you used to calculate your purchase price. I have found that once you prove to property owners that you have taken the time and effort to thoroughly research property values, they will realize that you are a serious and knowledgeable buyer who is not going to waste their time, and they will become more receptive to your offer.

Don't Be Bashful about Asking Property Owners to Help Finance the Purchase

First off, always ask property owners how much they want for their equity instead of how much they want for their property. This way, owners start to think in terms of how much equity they have in the property and not the overall sale price. Plus, you can follow this with my favorite question: Would you be willing to lend me your equity in the property secured by a seller-financed mortgage loan? Generally, I buy options on properties only from owners who are willing to help finance the purchase by providing seller-financed mortgage loans on reasonable terms. This way, owners lend you their equity, secured by a seller-financed mortgage or deed of trust loan on the property, which allows you to purchase it without going through the rigmarole of having to:

1. Fill out overly intrusive loan applications.
2. Qualify for new mortgage or deed of trust loans.
3. Pay outrageous loan fees.
4. Pay rip-off third-party due diligence fees.
5. Deal with less-than-honest lenders.

What to Do When a Property Owner Rejects Your Initial Offer to Buy an Option

You must understand that when you make unsolicited offers to purchase options on properties that are not advertised as being for sale, there is a better than 50 percent chance that your initial offer will be rejected. In fact, I consider a 5-to-10 ratio—which means that for every 10 property owners you approach, 5 will accept your offer—to buy an option probably to be overly optimistic. My acceptance ratio is more like 2 to 10. And this is why, to be successful in this business, you must learn how to overcome property owners' objections and outright rejection of your offer to buy an option. The best way that I know to do this is to become consistently persistent by sending owners brief follow-up letters every 30 days stating that you are still interested in buying an option on their property. You want to maintain contact with property owners who initially reject your offer to buy an option because their situations and circumstances can change in an instant, and your offer, which was rejected out of hand last month, may be perfectly acceptable this month. I am very persistent, and I once sent a property owner 10 follow-up letters before she sold me a low-cost option. The reason for her change of heart had nothing to do with me directly. Her sister, who lived in Georgia, became sick, and she had to move there to take care of her. It just so happened that she received my tenth letter on the very same day that she was notified of her sister's illness. And because I had not rolled over and given up when my first offer was shot down, I was able to realize a fast $15,000 profit for my resolve and stick-to-itiveness!

CHAPTER 14

How to Prepare Your Option Agreement So That You Are Fully Protected during the Option Period

The best way to protect your position as optionee during the option period is to have a well-written real estate option agreement, which clearly defines in plain English, without the usual legal gobbledygook, all of the terms, conditions, and provisions of the agreement, along with the rights and responsibilities of both the optionee and the optionor. The problem that I have with standard boilerplate real estate option agreements is that they are generally written in favor of the optionor and provide little or no protection for the rights of the optionee. For example, most run-of-the-mill option agreements never cover what happens to the option consideration fee paid by the optionee in the event that:

1. The property under option is condemned via eminent domain.
2. The property under option is destroyed by fire, storm, flood, earthquake, or terrorist attack.
3. The optionor defaults on the agreement by refusing to sell the property under option after the real estate option has been exercised.

Nineteen Clauses That Must Be Included in Your Option Agreement

One of the biggest mistakes that I made when I first started out as a real estate option investor was that I did not include clauses in my option agreements that fully protected my rights and interests as optionee. However, I started to wise up when a property I had an option on burned to the ground, and I was left with nothing but a pile of ashes to show for my $2,500 option fee. At this point, I quickly came to the realization that I had better include a clause in my option agreement that the option consideration fee would be refunded in the event the property under option was damaged or destroyed by fire. And over the years, I have refined and tweaked my real estate option agreement so that it now includes the following 19 optionee protection clauses:

1. *Parties to the agreement:* Designate all parties to the real estate option agreement as optionee and optionor to include their legal status as to whether single individual, husband and wife, or a business entity such as a corporation or limited liability company.

2. *Legal description of property:* Use the exact legal description that's written on the recorded deed of the property being put under option to describe it in the option agreement.

3. *Option to purchase:* Specify that the optionor grant the optionee the exclusive, unrestricted and irrevocable right and option to purchase the optionor's property.

4. *Option fee:* Include the full amount paid as the option fee and state that it is to be credited toward the purchase price when the option is exercised.

5. *Option period:* State the exact length of the real estate option period by calendar dates.

6. *Purchase price:* Specify the full purchase price of the property under option including how the purchase is to be financed.

7. *Exercise of option:* Outline exactly how the optionee is to exercise the real estate option including the method for notifying the optionor.

8. *Extension of option period:* State the optionee's right to extend the option period including the length and cost of each extension period.

9. *Assignment of option agreement:* Include a clause that gives the optionee the right to assign or sell the real estate option agreement to a third party.

10. *Waste clause:* Include a waste clause requiring the optionor to maintain the property during the option period.

11. *Default by optionee:* Specify that the consideration paid as the option fee is the sole and exclusive remedy in the event that the optionee exercises the option but fails to purchase the property.

12. *Default by optionor:* State that the optionee shall have the right of specific performance in the event that the optionor defaults by refusing to sell the property after the option has been exercised.

13. *Eminent domain:* Specify that the optionee will receive a full refund of the option fee plus any accrued interest if the property is condemned by eminent domain during the option period.

14. *Right of entry:* Include the optionee's right, upon notifying the optionor, to enter, clean, repair, market, and show the property during the option period.

15. *Risk of loss:* Specify that the optionee is entitled to a full refund of the option fee plus accrued interest if the property is damaged or destroyed by fire, storms, or earthquakes during the option period.

16. *Further encumbrances:* State that the optionor is prohibited from placing any additional encumbrances such as mortgage or deed of trust loans against the property during the option period.

17. *Title transfer documents:* State that a warranty or grant deed and purchase agreement with the notarized signature of the optionor are to be held in escrow by a reputable attorney or title or escrow company during the option period.

18. *Recording of memorandum of option:* If permitted by a state's recording statute, specify that the optionor execute and acknowledge a memorandum of real estate option agreement suitable for recording in the county's official public records where the title to the property under option is recorded.

19. *Option agreement to ripen into purchase agreement:* If you do not want to use a separate purchase agreement to buy the property after exercising the option, specify that in the event the option is exercised, the real estate option agreement shall automatically ripen into a purchase agreement without further notice.

The Definition of a Real Estate Option Agreement

In general legal terms, a *real estate option agreement* is a unilateral agreement, binding only on the optionor or seller, in which a promise—the exclusive, unrestricted, and irrevocable right and option to purchase—is exchanged for performance—the exercising of the option by the optionee or buyer. And the purchase of a real estate option does not impose any obligation on the optionee to exercise the option and purchase the property. However, once the optionee exercises the real estate option, the agreement becomes a bilateral contract binding on both parties, at which time the optionee becomes the buyer and the optionor, the seller. For example, in Florida, a real estate option agreement is distinguished from a purchase agreement in that no equitable interest passes to the optionee until after the real estate option is exercised. Once exercised, the real estate option agreement ripens into a bilateral purchase agreement.

Essential Elements of a Real Estate Option Agreement

The three essential elements that make a real estate option agreement valid are:

1. A specified real estate option period.
2. A clearly defined method for exercising the real estate option.
3. Valuable consideration paid as a real estate option fee by the optionee.

Your Option Agreement Must Comply with Your State's Real Property Statutes

First things first: Make certain that all the provisions in your real estate option agreement are in full compliance with all of your state's real property statutes. And whatever you do, do not operate under the false assumption that a real estate option agreement that you can download for free from a web site on the Internet is legal in your state. It most likely is not! This is because real estate contract law varies from state to state, and a real estate option agreement that is perfectly legal in Florida may include provisions that are considered unconscionable in Wisconsin. I cannot overemphasize the financial consequences that a poorly written real estate option agreement can have, especially when put under the scrutiny of a judge presiding over a lawsuit filed by a disgruntled optionor. For example, suppose that, after signing the option agreement, an optionor discovered that your real estate option agreement contained provisions that are considered to be unconscionable in your state, are illegal, and are not enforceable in a court of law. And now, the optionor has filed a lawsuit against you, the sleazy real estate investor, for damages, claiming that you took unfair advantage of him or her. However, since ignorance of the law is not considered to be a valid legal defense, you now have little choice but to try to settle out of court with the optionor before the case goes to trial. A state-by-state listing of real property statutes that are currently available online can be found at the following web site: www.law.cornell.edu/topics/state_statutes3.html#property.

Hire an Experienced, Board-Certified Real Estate Attorney in Good Standing

To avoid being snookered by some incompetent $300-an-hour attorney in an Armani suit and alligator shoes masquerading as a real estate attorney, I very highly recommend that you proceed with caution when selecting a real estate attorney. You must hire an honest, competent, board-certified real estate attorney in good standing, who has experience working with real estate options. Once your attorney is hired, his or her job is to advise you on the proper preparation of your real estate option agreement. A word of warning: Please do not ignore the very sage advice that I am dispensing here and use the services of an attorney specializing in divorce law to advise you on real estate options. You must hire the services of an experienced, board-certified real estate attorney in good standing who:

1. Specializes in the daily practice of real estate law.
2. Is well versed on how real estate option transactions work in your state.
3. Has ample experience preparing real estate option agreements.
4. Knows how to insure real estate options properly with title insurance.
5. Is affiliated with a reputable title insurance underwriter.
6. Is licensed to sell title insurance in your state.

The Standard Qualifications for an Attorney to Be Certified in Real Estate Law

In most states, attorneys in good standing are defined as: "those persons licensed to practice law who have paid annual state bar association membership dues for the current year and who are not retired, resigned, delinquent, inactive, or suspended members of the state bar association." The basic qualifications for attorneys to be certified in real estate law are pretty standard nationwide. For example, the Florida Bar Association requires that every attorney certified in real estate law must have practiced law for at least five years, with 40 percent or more of his or her time spent in the practice of real estate law during the three years immediately preceding application for certification. In addition, attorneys applying for certification must have passed a peer review, completed 45 hours of continuing legal education within the three years immediately preceding the application, and passed a written examination.

How to Find a Board-Certified Real Estate Attorney in Your Area

The best way to find a qualified, board-certified real estate attorney in your area is to contact your local bar association lawyer referral service or your state's bar association lawyer referral service. Once you have the names of board-certified real estate attorneys in your area, you'll need to do an online search of your state's bar association membership rolls to verify that the attorneys on your list are licensed to practice law in your state and to see whether they've been disciplined or had their license revoked for misconduct. The following three web sites provide online attorney locator services that allow you to search for an attorney by specialty and location:

Martindale Hubbell Lawyer Locator: www.martindale.com/locator/home.html

Findlaw: www.findlaw.com/14firms

Lawyers: www.lawyers.com

Use the Option Agreement That Your Attorney Prepared as Your Master Copy

Once you have your initial real estate option agreement properly prepared by a board-certified real estate attorney, use it as your master copy so you will not have to go running back to your real estate attorney for a new real estate option agreement every time you buy an option. You can use the option agreement your attorney prepared for you and just change the optionor's name, date of option period, option fee amount, purchase price, option extension periods, and cost, along with the property's street address and legal description.

Make Certain That All Your Real Estate Agreements Are Properly Witnessed

You must make certain that the signatures on a real estate agreement or memorandum of agreement are properly witnessed because documents that are not properly witnessed are not in what is known as a recordable form. This means that the document cannot be recorded in the official public records. Each state has its own requirement as to the number of witnesses that are needed to attest the signatures on documents affecting real property. For example, in Florida, two witnesses are required to attest the signatures on real property transaction and title transfer documents.

In addition to having the signatures on all your real estate agreements properly witnessed, you must have the signatures on all your real estate agreements notarized by a state licensed notary public. Real estate agreements with signatures that are not properly acknowledged by a licensed notary public cannot be recorded in the official public records. And unrecorded documents have no effect on the title to real property.

All Sample Agreements Are for Informational and Instructional Purposes Only

Please note that I have included sample real estate option, memorandum of real estate option, and purchase agreements in this book for informational and instructional purposes only. For specific information on how to properly document a real estate option transaction in your state, please follow my advice and consult with a board-certified real estate attorney who is licensed to practice law in your state. A sample real estate option agreement follows.

FORM 14.1 Sample Real Estate Option Agreement

This real estate option is given on this ninth day of July 2005, by David D. Jones, a single man, known hereinafter as the Optionor, to Donald S. Reed, a single man, known hereinafter as the Optionee. Optionor, in consideration of the sum of ten thousand dollars ($10,000), paid by Optionee to Optionor, grants to Optionee the exclusive, unrestricted, and irrevocable right and option to purchase, on the following terms and conditions, that certain real property known as: 45735 Hillsborough Avenue, Tampa, Florida 33603, and legally described as: Lots 47, 48, and 49 of Carters subdivision according to map or plat thereof as recorded in plat book 69, page 89, of the public records of Hillsborough County, Florida.

In the event Optionee shall exercise the option, the consideration paid for the option shall be applied against the purchase price. If Optionee does not exercise the option, Optionor shall be entitled to retain the consideration paid for the option as complete compensation for the option, and no portion thereof shall be refunded to Optionee.

The purchase price of the property is three hundred and fifty thousand dollars ($350,000), which amount will be paid if Optionee elects to exercise this real estate option.

If this real estate option is exercised, Optionor, as Seller, and Optionee or assigns, as Buyer, shall perform the Purchase Agreement attached hereto as addendum one (1).

This option is effective immediately and will expire at 12:01 a.m. on July 8, 2006.

(continued)

FORM 14.1 **Sample Real Estate Option Agreement** *(Continued)*

Optionee or assigns may exercise this real estate option only by delivering a written notice thereof, signed by Optionee, or assigns, to Optionor before the time herein set for expiration. Any such notice must be sent by United States Postal Service Certified Mail, return receipt requested, or personal delivery to the post office address of Optionor, which is 5300 West Oklahoma Avenue, Tampa, Florida 33629.

Optionee or assigns shall have the right to extend the option period provided herein for two additional periods of twelve (12) months each by giving written notice thereof to Optionor, and upon payment to Optionor the sum of four thousand five hundred dollars ($4,500) for the first extension period, and the sum of four thousand five hundred dollars ($4,500) for the second extension period, provided the notice is given and the sums of money are paid in full to Optionor prior to the expiration of the option period, or extension thereof immediately preceding the additional extension period requested.

If Optionee or assigns do not exercise this option in accordance with its terms and within the option period and any extension thereof, this option and all rights of Optionee or assigns shall automatically and immediately terminate without notice and Optionor shall have no further obligation to Optionee.

Optionor shall not further encumber the optioned property during the period of the option, nor shall any existing lease be extended, or any new lease entered into without Optionee's express written consent. In the event any lien or other encumbrance is placed upon the property during the option period, Optionor shall immediately cause same to be removed at Optionor's sole expense. Failure to remove the encumbrance within thirty (30) days after notice is given to Optionor by Optionee shall constitute a breach of this option agreement, and Optionee shall have all remedies for damages provided by law, or in equity, or at the sole option of Optionee. Optionee may elect to require Optionor to return all consideration paid to Optionor plus eighteen percent (18%) interest thereon and cancel this Real Estate Option Agreement, and in such event, neither party shall have any further obligation hereunder.

Optionor shall maintain the property during the period of this agreement in the same condition it existed as of the date of this agreement, ordinary wear and tear excepted.

In the event that during the option period, all or any substantial portion of the property shall be taken for condemnation, or under the right of eminent domain, Optionee shall be entitled to a full refund of all consideration paid to Optionor, if Optionee fails to exercise the option. In addition, Optionor shall reimburse Optionee for any expense reasonably incurred by Optionee in examining title to the property, and other costs incidental thereto.

In the event of loss or damage by storm, fire, flood, earthquake, or terrorist attack to the improvements now existing on the premises of the property, during the option period, Optionee shall have the right to rescind this Real Estate Option Agreement, and shall be entitled to a full refund of all consideration paid to Optionor. In addition, Optionor shall reimburse Optionee for any expense reasonably incurred by Optionee in examining title to the property, and other costs incidental thereto.

Optionee and Optionee's assigns, agents, and employees shall have the unfettered right to enter onto the property during the period of the option to make improvements, show said property, and carry out other such work that may be necessary.

Optionee and Optionee's assigns, agents, and employees shall have the unfettered right to enter onto the property during the period of the option to make improvements, show said property, and carry out other such work that may be necessary.

Optionee or assigns shall have the unfettered right to act in the name of Optionor to apply for any regulatory, zoning, or property use variance that Optionee deems necessary for optionee's future use of the property.

Optionor agrees that should Optionee or assigns exercise the real estate option within the specified option period and subsequently fail to close the purchase in accordance with the terms of this Real Estate Option Agreement or for any reason other than failure of Optionor to tender marketable title, Optionor shall retain the total consideration paid for the option as full and complete liquidated damages, and neither party shall have any further responsibility under this Real Estate Option Agreement. The parties agree that their relationship under this Real Estate Option Agreement is that of Optionor and Optionee and that it shall not be deemed or interpreted to create between them the relationship of principal and agent, employer and employee, seller and purchaser, or partners.

All rights of the Optionee under this Real Estate Option Agreement are fully assignable without the consent of the Optionor.

Optionor and Optionee shall not record a copy of this Real Estate Option Agreement in the official public records, but in lieu thereof, and for the purpose of giving public notice, Optionor and Optionee agree to execute and acknowledge a Memorandum of Real Estate Option Agreement suitable for recordation in the official public records of Hillsborough County, Florida.

All provisions of this Real Estate Option Agreement shall extend to, bind, and inure to the benefit of heirs, executors, personal representatives, successors, and assigns of Optionor and Optionee.

Optionor and Optionee or assigns authorize Mr. John B. Good, Attorney at Law, to act as Escrow Agent to hold the Deed and Purchase Agreement signed by Optionor during the option period. If Optionee or assigns fail to exercise this real estate option in accordance with the terms of this Real Estate Option Agreement, Escrow Agent shall immediately return the signed Deed and Purchase Agreement to Optionor.

IN WITNESS WHEREOF, Optionor and Optionee have set their hands the date aforesaid.

David D. Jones	Donald S. Reed
Optionor	Optionee
Robert B. Big	Sally M. Little
Witness	Witness

CHAPTER 15

How to Use Title Insurance to Insure Real Estate Options

Most recorded ownership, leasehold, and contractual interests such as agreements for deed, contracts for deed, and other rights in real property can be insured with title insurance. As a general rule, if an interest or right in real property, such as a real estate option, is notarized and recorded in the official public records of the county where the property's title is recorded, it can be insured with an owner's title insurance policy. You need to understand that what you are really buying when you buy a real estate option is the property owner's equitable, leasehold, and contractual interests and rights in the title to the property that you are buying the option on. And because there are a number of factors that can affect a property's title and thus its marketability, you need to make certain that any property you buy an option on can be insured with an owner's title insurance policy, issued by a reputable title insurer. In most states, real estate option agreements can be insured by using a standard owner's title insurance policy with a real estate option endorsement. The real estate option endorsement insures the optionee's right to exercise the real estate option. It also insures the priority of the real estate option over any other liens that may be subsequently recorded against the property's title. But if you live in a state that does not recognize a real estate option as being a valid and insurable interest in real property, you will not be able to have your real estate option insured with an option endorsement. The only way that you, as an optionee, can insure a real estate option is with an owner's title insurance policy that includes a real estate option endorsement, which insures your real estate option agreement, rather than just the title of the property being put under option. However, most title insurers will recommend that real estate optionees buy only a standard owner's title insurance policy, which insures the title of the property being put under option, but not the actual real estate option itself. Do not do it. When you buy a title insurance policy to insure a real estate option, you pay a one-time insurance premium, and the insurance policy remains in effect for the life of the option. Typically, a real estate option endorsement policy insures the policyholder against future losses or damages resulting from any valid claims made against the insured property's title. In other words, the title insurer will pay all legal fees for defending any valid claims made against the insured property's title as long as the policyholder retains an interest or right in the property. For example, the standard American Land Title Association (ALTA) owners' title insurance policy provides policyholders with coverage against title defects that originated prior to the policy being issued. Common title defects covered in standard ALTA owners' title insurance policies include:

1. Errors, omissions, and insufficiencies in the abstract or title search.
2. Errors of judgment, negligence, and mistakes on the part of the title examiner.
3. Undisclosed errors and deficiencies in recorded documents, including the misfiling of recorded documents or improper indexing.
4. When not specifically excluded, errors in, or insufficiency of, the survey.
5. Forgeries within recorded documents.
6. Secret marriages or misrepresentations of marital status.
7. Unknown or undisclosed heirs.
8. False impersonation.
9. Instruments executed under expired or revoked powers of attorney.
10. Mental incompetence of the parties executing documents.
11. Confusion due to similar or identical names.
12. Lack of authority of the federal or state government to dispose of or convey the insured property.
13. Children born after execution of a will.
14. Discovery of a will of an apparent intestate.
15. Easements by prescription, which were not disclosed by a land survey.

Why Most Title Insurers Consider Real Estate Options to Be Risky

Please keep in mind that title insurers, by the very nature of their business, are rather skittish when it comes to what they will insure. And to most title insurers, insuring real estate options is perceived as being risky business. Title insurers generally consider straight or naked real estate options, which are not contained in lease-options, to be more risky than so-called ordinary real estate instruments. Why the greater perceived risk with real estate options? There are many reasons. For example, all title insurers fear that an increase in the value of a property under option could cause an optionor to refuse to transfer the property's title after the real estate option has been exercised. In a nutshell, title insurers are leery about being held responsible for the potential cost involved to legally force an optionor to transfer the title to the property under option. Title insurers are also fearful that the title to a property under option may be owned by an individual who could become afflicted with some sort of disability, which would preclude the transfer of the property's title except by a potentially time-consuming and costly specific performance lawsuit.

What a Standard Real Estate Option Endorsement Doesn't Insure

Generally, a standard real estate option endorsement does not insure against loss or damage caused by:

1. Disaffirmance of the real estate option, under the provisions of the U.S. Bankruptcy Code. The interest of a real estate optionee is subject to being rejected as an executory contract under the U.S. Bankruptcy Code in the event the optionor files a bankruptcy petition.
2. The effect of any condemnation proceeding, including the failure of the optionee to receive all or part of an award entered in a condemnation proceeding, unless failure to share in the award stems solely from a court order or judgment, constituting a final determination that the option is invalid.
3. Any lien or right to a lien for services, labor, or material imposed by law.
4. Expenses required to enforce a real estate option and to obtain a transfer of title from the optionor and any other party holding title to any interest in the property at the time the option is exercised.
5. Expense of obtaining valid conveyances or release of any rights, interests, or liens related to the property that appear in the public records or are known to the insured at the time of exercising the real estate option.

What Title Insurers Look for in a Real Estate Option Agreement

Here is a listing of what title insurers look for when reviewing a real estate option agreement to determine its insurability:

1. Does the real estate option, prior to its being exercised, create an estate in land under state statutes?
2. Is the real estate option recordable under state statutes so that it constitutes constructive notice?
3. Does the real estate option violate any state statutes against perpetuities?
4. Does the real estate option clearly state the purchase price of the property being put under option?
5. Is the real estate option enforceable against third parties having actual or constructive notice under state statutes?
6. Is the optionee entitled under state statutes to be notified when any litigation is instituted against the title of the property being put under option?

Always Obtain Title Insurance Coverage from a Reputable National Underwriter

A title insurance policy, like all types of insurance policies, is only as good as the company underwriting it. So, when you buy any type of title insurance, always use the services of a board-certified real estate attorney or a title or escrow agent whose title insurance policies are underwritten by a reputable regional or national underwriter, such as First American Title Insurance Company, Chicago Title & Trust Company, Lawyers Title Insurance Corporation, Old Republic Title Insurance Company, Fidelity National Title Insurance Company, or Stewart Title Insurance Company. However, I must warn you that most title and escrow agents are totally clueless when it comes to knowing anything about straight real estate options. This is why I highly recommend that you purchase title insurance through a board-certified real estate attorney or reputable title insurance company that has a competent real estate attorney on the staff of its underwriting department. Once you have the names of local attorneys or title insurers or escrow companies, you need to contact each office to get the name, title, and mailing address of the person in charge of the underwriting department. Then, you need to send each one a short letter like the sample on page 170, which briefly states that you are a real estate option investor who wants to insure your real estate options with an option endorsement.

Get a Title Insurance Policy Commitment before Buying a Real Estate Option

Prior to ever buying a real estate option, you need to first contact a reputable attorney or title insurance or escrow company and have them perform a title

FORM 15.1   Sample Letter to Title Insurers

July 7, 2005

Ms. Paula Patterson
Manager
Underwriting Department
XYZ Title Insurance Company
5600 Del Cruise Way
Orlando, FL 32867

Dear Ms. Patterson,

I am a real estate investor who buys real estate options on residential and commercial property located in the Greater Orlando area.

I am currently in search of a competent title insurance agency that represents a reputable title insurance underwriter who insures straight real estate options, which are not part of a leasehold interest.

Specifically, I am looking for a company with a knowledgeable and experienced underwriting staff in house, which is capable of making quick decisions regarding insurability issues.

Please contact me by e-mail at rpfrazier@juno.com at your earliest convenience to set up an appointment so that we may discuss my title insurance requirements in detail.

Thank you for your prompt response.

Sincerely,

Ronald P. Frazier

search to determine if they will issue an owner's title insurance policy commitment to insure the property's title. You must do this so you do not waste your valuable time pursuing potential option properties with titles that are riddled with title defects that cannot be quickly and inexpensively cured. An owner's title insurance policy commitment, sometimes referred to as a *binder*, is a temporary insurance contract providing for the future issuance of a permanent owner's title insurance policy after a valid instrument such as a deed, contract, or agreement for deed, lease, or real estate option creating an insurable interest or right in real property is executed, delivered, and recorded. I know an option investor in Manchester, New Hampshire, who once made the mistake of buying an option on a small, non-working dairy farm without first getting a title insurance policy commitment from a title insurer. And to make matters worse, this guy did not even have a title search done before he shelled out $15,000 for a one-year option. When he did contact a title insurer about insuring his option, they did a title search and found out that the husband and wife who were listed on the deed as the owners of record had five adult children who had recorded quit claim deeds from their parents, giving each one of them a 10 percent interest in the property. However, all of the children had left the state and had not spoken to good old Mom and Dad for over 10 years. Given the circumstances surrounding the property's fractured ownership, no title insurance company would touch it with a 10-foot pole. The investor eventually found two of the children, but they basically told him to drop dead. He now refers to this little episode as his $15,000 option seminar!

Three Factors to Always Consider before Insuring an Option

The very first thing that I do after I have done my preliminary due diligence and determined that the property owner is willing to sell me an option is to have a title search done on the property's title by a seasoned title professional who has experience doing title searches in public records libraries for title insurance companies. I do this so that my title expert can determine if the property's title is in an insurable condition. Once I know the status of the property's title, I consider the following three factors before deciding whether to buy title insurance to insure my real estate option:

1. *The property owner's background and reputation:* Property owners who are considered sophisticated professionals, such as medical doctors, dentists, attorneys, engineers, and business executives, are generally more likely to

be litigious than owners from different backgrounds. The same holds true for properties owned by business entities controlled by the same type of professionals. Also included in this group of owners to be wary of are owners who have a reputation for being difficult to deal with. If a property owner falls within this group, I insure my option with title insurance.

2. *The cost of the option:* When the option fee is $10,000 or more, I insure my option.

3. *The purchase price of the property:* I buy title insurance on my option when the purchase price of the property is $250,000 or more.

In case you did not know it, title insurance is not cheap! And that is exactly why I do not just go out and get title insurance on every option that I buy. For example, here in Florida, an owner's title insurance policy on a residential property valued at $175,000 costs $950. So, for options that cost less than $10,000 on properties valued at less than $150,000 that do not belong to sue-happy owners, I forgo insuring the option. And to date, knock on wood, I have never had an owner renege on our option agreement by refusing to sell the property after the option was exercised.

Title Insurance Underwriting Information Available Online

Title insurance underwriting information and real estate option endorsement forms are available online at the following web sites:

Old Republic National Title Insurance Company: http://orlink.oldrepnatl.com /Underwriters/pages/Table%20of%20Contents.htm

Chicago Title Insurance Company: www.ctic.com/operations.htm

First American Title Insurance Company: www.firstam.com/faf/reference /uwtools.html

Stewart Title Virtual Underwriter: www.vuwriter.com

Why All Property Title Transfer Documents Must Be Held in Escrow during the Option Period

A word of warning: The longer you stay in this business, there is a better than 50 percent chance that you are going to unknowingly buy a real estate option from a dishonest property owner who will try to renege on your option agreement. Granted, this is an integrity problem, which harkens back to the old adage: Any agreement is only as good as the people who sign it. However, this is exactly what happens all too often to uninformed option investors who end up getting ripped off by unscrupulous optionors who take their option money but later renege on the real estate option agreement by failing to sell the property under option after the option is exercised. Nevertheless, this potential problem is easily avoidable when all the property transfer documents are signed by the optionor and witnessed in the presence of a notary public and held in escrow by a reputable third party during the option period. In this way, whoever exercises the option can purchase the property without first having to get the optionor to sign a real estate purchase agreement and a warranty or grant deed transferring the title to the property. Plus, as you will find out, having all of the title transfer documents signed, sealed, and ready for delivery is a tremendous selling point when you want to assign a real estate option agreement to a third party.

Over the years, I have had only one optionor renege on a real estate option agreement by refusing to sell the property under option after I had exercised my option. Please note that this occurred before I smartened up and required that all title transfer documents be signed by the optionor at the same time that the option agreement is signed. Let me start off by saying that the optionor who pulled this stunt would never be confused with a candidate for a Rhodes scholarship. I mailed him an exercise of real estate option notification letter, in full compliance with the terms of our option agreement, which was just like the sample in Chapter 20 (page 207). I sent the notification letter via U.S. Postal Service Certified Mail, return receipt requested, and he personally signed for it. And when I called him on the telephone after I did not receive a response from him to confirm the closing date, he had the gall to tell me that he had never received anything from me in the mail. Furthermore, he stated something to the effect that pigs would fly before he would ever sell the property to me for the previously agreed-upon sale price. Needless to say, I was not a happy camper! I reviewed my options and decided that my best course of action would be to file a small claims lawsuit against him in Hillsborough County Small Claims Court to recover my $2,000 option fee and court costs. I went ahead and filed my lawsuit and the optionor failed to show up in court, and I obtained a default judgment against him for $2,178, which I had recorded against the title of each of the five parcels of land that he owned in Hillsborough County, Florida. A couple of months later, this swell guy left a profanity-laced message on my telephone answering machine, threatening to have me arrested for placing judgment liens against his properties. The following week, I received a cashier's check for $2,200 from his attorney, along with a request that I return a notarized satisfaction of lien as soon as possible. I promptly cashed the check and sent the former optionor a completed satisfaction of lien, on which I purposely did not have my signature notarized. The optionor had a conniption fit when he received the nonrecordable satisfaction of lien and telephoned me and once again threatened to have me arrested. I told him to buzz off! And 30 days later, in full accordance with the Florida statutes, Mr. Slicky-Boy received a recordable satisfaction of lien from me.

The Four Documents That Must Be Signed and Held in Escrow

If you do not learn anything else from this chapter, please learn this: Without exception, require that the following property title transfer documents be signed by the optionor, witnessed, and notarized:

1. One copy of the real estate option agreement with witnessed and notarized signatures of the optionor and optionee.
2. One copy of the addendum Real Estate Purchase Agreement, like the sample in Chapter 20 (page 210), with the witnessed and notarized signature of the optionor as seller only, with the buyer's name and signature left blank in case the option agreement is assigned to a third party.

3. One copy of the warranty or grant deed, with the witnessed and notarized signature of the optionor as grantor and with the grantee's name left blank in case the option agreement is assigned to a third party.

4. Two copies of the HUD 1 Settlement Statement, listing the buyer's and seller's closing costs. For your information, there is a fillable HUD 1 Settlement Statement on my web site, www.thomaslucier.com.

Also, prior to having the optionor sign the title transfer documents, take the time to double-check them for mistakes in:

1. Transposing numbers and letters.
2. Spelling and typing.
3. Calculating the closing costs.

I always have the optionor sign the title transfer documents at the same time the real estate option agreement is signed and witnessed in the presence of a notary public. I then have all the property title transfer documents held in escrow by a reputable third party during the option period. This way, once the real estate option is exercised, all the documents necessary to close on the purchase of the property under option will have already been signed, witnessed, and notarized. Doing this eliminates any last-minute scurrying around to get the optionor to sign the paperwork to close the deal and makes buying the property under option simply a matter of going to the designated attorney or title or escrow agent with the funds necessary to close on the purchase. Most important for you, however, or for whoever buys your real estate option, doing this will eliminate any possibility that the optionor can renege on your real estate option agreement by refusing to sell the property after the option has been exercised. In fact, if you follow the advice that I am giving you here, there will be no need for you to ever meet with the optionor again. On my last six option deals, I have never had a face-to-face meeting with the optionor. All six deals were negotiated via telephone and e-mail, and all of the title transfer documents were signed out of state in the presence of a notary public and returned to the third-party escrow agent via U.S. Postal Service Express Mail.

Once these four documents are signed by the optionor and sealed by a notary public, have them held in escrow by a reputable third party, such as a real estate attorney or title or escrow agent, during the option period. This way, all the property title transfer documents are at one location and:

1. Readily available for review by potential assignees and buyers who may doubt their existence.

2. Readily available for review by mortgage lenders financing the purchase of the property.
3. Readily available to facilitate a fast closing for whoever exercises the real estate option.

Why a Signed Warranty or Grant Deed Is Better Than a Performance Mortgage

Some investors advocate using a performance mortgage or deed of trust to secure the performance of an optionor under a real estate option agreement. However, I do not recommend using a performance mortgage or deed of trust for the following two reasons:

1. Most property owners will refuse to sign a performance mortgage or deed of trust.
2. Foreclosing on a performance mortgage or deed of trust can be very time consuming and costly.

As far as I am concerned, an optionee has no better security than a warranty or grant deed that is being held in escrow by a reputable third party and bears the witnessed and notarized signature of the optionor as grantor. Once the optionor signs a warranty or grant deed as the grantor, there is no legal way that he or she can default on the real estate option agreement later on by refusing to sell the property under option.

Why You Should Record a Memorandum of Real Estate Option Agreement

In addition to having all the title transfer documents held in escrow during the option period, I think that given human nature and the greed factor, you would have to be brain-dead not to record a memorandum of real estate option. Recording a memorandum of real estate option agreement like the sample in Chapter 17 (page 183) against the title to the property under option provides constructive notice to the public that you have a valid real estate option to purchase the property. However, not all state statutes allow a memorandum of real estate option agreement to be recorded. In most states, in order to be recorded, a real estate option must establish a valid interest or right in the property being put under option. Check with the supervisor or manager of your county's public recorder's office to determine if a memorandum of real estate option agreement can be recorded in the official public records of your county.

CHAPTER 17

How to Close on the Purchase of a Real Estate Option

Nothing happens in this business until an investor actually puts a piece of property under option. This is the first step that all would-be option investors must be willing to take if they are really serious about making money with real estate options! In this chapter, you will learn all of the do's and don'ts of how to close on the purchase of a real estate option. I also tell you how to avoid the common closing mistakes that most uninformed investors make, which can come back to haunt you later when you are trying to resell or exercise your option. The trick to having a smooth closing is to have all of the details of the transaction hammered out and finalized before you and the optionor ever sit down together at the closing table. This way, the optionor will not be able to try to renegotiate the terms of your option agreement at the closing. I once had an optionor who showed up at a closing and refused to sign our option agreement until I upped the option fee another $3,000. I quickly informed this guy that I was not in the business of negotiating with extortionists and that he could either honor our previously agreed-on option price or take a hike. Once he realized that I was not going to allow myself to be shaken down, he quickly backed off his demand and signed every single piece of paper that was put in front of him.

If you follow my advice in Chapter 16, you will have all of the title transfer documents prepared by your attorney prior to the closing date. This way, all the optionor has to do is to show up at closing and sign his or her name in the presence of a notary public. You can then have the documents held in escrow during the option period by your attorney or closing agent. Doing this will totally eliminate the possibility of the optionor reneging on the option agreement later on by failing to sell the property after the option has been exercised.

What to Do If the Optionor Refuses to Sign All of the Documents at the Closing

During negotiations and prior to the closing, you must explain to the optionor that he or she will have to sign the title transfer documents for the property—real estate purchase agreement and warranty or grant deed—at the same time the option agreement is signed. I have found that if you make it clear from the very beginning of negotiations that signing all the property title transfer documents is part of the transaction, this will not become a deal-killer later on. And it has been my experience that if you act in a competent professional manner and do everything exactly as you say you are going to do it, you will gain the trust of most reasonable property owners. The investors who have the most problems with optionors are the ones who come across as slick wheeler-dealer types and have a hard time giving people a straight answer. However, when an optionor does change his or her mind and refuses to sign the real estate option agreement, addendum real estate purchase agreement, and a warranty or grant deed at the closing, you need to find out exactly why he or she is refusing to do so. In most cases, you will hear some excuse about how he or she does not trust any attorney or title or escrow agent to hold the documents. Or, optionors will claim that they are afraid that you are going to "steal their property right out from under their nose." If this is the case, tell the optionor you will not be able to buy an option on the property unless he or she agrees to sign the property title transfer documents.

Whatever you do, never, ever fork over any money for an option without first getting the optionor's acknowledged signature on all of the title transfer documents. I once received a frantic telephone call from an option investor in Bakersfield, California, who made the mistake of not getting the optionor to sign the property's title transfer documents at the same time the option agreement was signed. According to the investor, the optionor appeared to be a "sweet old lady," who had told him that she was a retired schoolteacher. So, he figured he had nothing to worry about and did not ask her to sign title transfer documents. Well, lo and behold, three months later, when he notified her that he wanted to exercise his option and buy the property, she told him in no uncertain terms what he could do with his option. He told me that he felt like the world's biggest fool. I told him to record his option agreement against the property's title and to send her a letter threatening a lawsuit if she did not refund his $5,000 option fee within 48 hours. I do not know how it turned out as I never heard back from him. But I do know that all of this could have been easily avoided if he had insisted that all of the title transfer documents be signed at the closing.

All Signatures on Real Estate Transaction Documents Must Be Properly Witnessed

To reiterate what I told you in Chapter 14, you can have the best option agreement known to mankind, but if the signatures of both the optionee and optionor are not properly witnessed, the agreement will most likely be unenforceable in a court of law. This can become a real problem when an unscrupulous optionor decides, for whatever reason, that he or she wants out of your option agreement. When this happens, you can bet your bippy that the optionor or his or her attorney will be going over your agreement with a fine-tooth comb in search for any way to weasel out of it. And an option agreement with flawed signatures would provide the weasel with a legal way out of the deal. You also need to know that property title transfer documents, such as a warranty or grant deed, with signatures that have not been properly witnessed and acknowledged by a notary public cannot be recorded in the public records of the county where the property's title is recorded. In other words, a deed with flawed signatures, which was not signed in the presence of a notary public, is absolutely worthless.

Why It's Best to Use a Board-Certified Real Estate Attorney to Close Transactions

There seems to be a common misconception among the real estate buying and selling public that title or escrow agents always look out for the best interests of all parties involved in a transaction. However, the fact of the matter is that title and escrow agents are trained to act in the best interest of their companies and the title insurer. They have no fiduciary obligation to the principal parties involved in any type of real estate transaction. In other words, when you are a principal in a real estate transaction in which a title or escrow agent is acting as the closing agent, there is no one but you looking out for your best interests. The only thing that the title or escrow agent is concerned about is that all the closing documents are signed and that the proceeds from the sale are disbursed. And I can tell you from my own experiences that I have found most title and escrow companies are not exactly what I would call investor-friendly. The reason for the cold-shoulder treatment is probably that most title insurance and escrow companies are generally leery of doing business with anyone they perceive as being unconventional. By the very nature of their business, title and escrow companies are generally suspicious of any type of real estate transaction that involves more than a typical, run-of-the-mill, easy-to-close residential sale with a buyer and seller and two real estate agents. The average title or escrow agent does not understand how real estate option transactions are structured. And like most people, they fear what they fail to understand. This fear factor that most title and escrow companies seem to have about real estate investors fosters an atmosphere of mistrust, which is not conducive to a good working relationship. This is why I highly recommend that you follow the advice I gave you in Chapter 14 and hire an honest, competent, board-certified real estate attorney to act as your legal counsel and closing agent in all real estate transactions. This way, you will have someone working for you who:

1. Has a working knowledge of real property statutory regulations and case law.
2. Is experienced in solving complex legal problems related to real property.
3. Understands the mechanics of a real estate option transaction.
4. Has a fiduciary obligation to act in his or her client's best interest.

Provide Joint Escrow Instructions to the Third Party Holding the Documents

The only surefire way that I know of to avoid any confusion or misinterpretations on the part of anyone involved in a real estate option transaction is to provide detailed, written escrow instructions, like the sample on page 181, to the attorney or title or escrow agent who is acting as the closing agent and holding the title transfer documents in escrow during the option period. The joint escrow instructions must be witnessed and signed by both the optionor and the optionee and notarized. List all of the documents to be held in escrow during the option period. In addition, the escrow instructions outline exactly what is to happen when the real estate option is:

1. Assigned.
2. Extended.
3. Exercised.
4. Expired.

Why You Should Record a Memorandum of Real Estate Option Agreement

Finally, I highly recommend that you include a clause in your real estate option agreement that allows you to record a memorandum of real estate option

FORM 17.1   Sample Joint Escrow Instructions

On this ninth day of July 2005, Robert D. Jones as Optionor/Seller and Donald S. Reed as Optionee/Buyer agree to have Mr. John B. Good, attorney at law, whose law office is located at 6907 Charleston Court, Tampa, Florida 33607, hold the following documents in escrow for the period from July 9, 2005 to 12:01 A.M. on July 8, 2006:

1. One copy of the Real Estate Option Agreement dated July 9, 2005, with the witnessed and notarized signatures of the Optionor and Optionee.

2. One copy of the addendum Real Estate Purchase Agreement, with the witnessed and notarized signature of the Optionor as Seller only.

3. One copy of the Warranty Deed with the witnessed and notarized signature of the Optionor as grantor.

4. Two copies of the HUD 1 Settlement Statement, which lists the Buyer's and Seller's closing costs.

The documents listed above are to be held in escrow by Mr. Good, in accordance with the following joint escrow instructions:

1. All notices to Mr. Jones, Mr. Reed, and Mr. Good must be sent by United States Postal Service Certified Mail, return receipt requested.

2. In the event that the Real Estate Option Agreement is assigned to a third party, Mr. Reed must send Mr. Jones and Mr. Good one copy each of the Real Estate Option Assignment Agreement along with the full legal name and post office address of the assignee.

3. In the event that the real estate option period is extended, Mr. Reed or his assigns must send Mr. Good a copy of the option extension notice with witnessed and notarized signatures of Mr. Jones and Mr. Reed or his assigns.

4. In the event that the real estate option is exercised, Mr. Reed or his assigns must send Mr. Jones an exercise of real estate option notice. A copy of the notice also must be sent to Mr. Good.

5. Mr. Reed or his assigns must execute the Real Estate Purchase Agreement held in escrow by Mr. Good, by having his signature as Buyer witnessed and notarized.

6. Mr. Reed or his assigns must provide Mr. Good with a cashier's check in United States currency that is drawn on a local bank and made payable to Mr. Jones, in the amount stipulated in the Real Estate Purchase Agreement, less the Seller's closing costs and any additional adjustments or prorations.

7. Mr. Reed or his assigns shall receive the Warranty Deed held in escrow by Mr. Good.

8. Mr. Good must send Mr. Jones his cashier's check and copies of the HUD 1 Settlement Statement and Warranty Deed within twenty-four hours of the transaction closing.

(continued)

9.   In the event the option period expires without the option being exercised, Mr. Good must send Mr. Jones the Real Estate Purchase Agreement and Warranty Deed within twenty-four hours of the expiration date.

IN WITNESS WHEREOF, Optionor/Seller and Optionee/Buyer have set their hands the date aforesaid.

David D. Jones   Donald S. Reed
Optionor   Optionee

Robert B. Big   Sally M. Little
Witness   Witness

agreement, such as the sample on page 183, in the public record of the county where the deed to the property under option is recorded. I advise recording a memorandum instead of the actual real estate option agreement because the terms of the agreement should be kept confidential. There is no reason to tell your competitors what you are up to. When I was young and dumb, I learned the hard way about not recording a memorandum of option in the public records. A property that I owned an option on was condemned by an eminent domain action by the Florida Department of Transportation as part of a road-widening project. But because I had failed to record a memorandum of option in the public records of the county where the property was located, the State of Florida had no way of knowing that I owned an option on the property, and I was never notified. However, if I had recorded a memorandum of option, I would have been notified by the state of Florida and could have exercised my option, bought the property, and walked away with a nice payday! Instead, I ended up learning about the eminent domain proceeding after my option had expired.

FORM 17.2   Sample Memorandum of Real Estate Option Agreement

---

This Memorandum of Real Estate Option Agreement made this ninth day of July 2005 is for the purpose of recording and giving notice of a Real Estate Option Agreement between Donald S. Reed, a single man, as the Optionee, in which the Optionor, David Jones, a single man, grants to Optionee the exclusive, unrestricted, and irrevocable right and option to purchase that certain real property known as: 45735 Hillsborough Avenue, Tampa, Florida 33603, and legally described as: Lots 47, 48, and 49 of Carters subdivision, according to map or plat thereof, as recorded in plat book 69, page 89, of the public records of Hillsborough County, Florida, that was executed between the Optionor and Optionee on the ninth day of July 2005 and which will expire at 12:01 a.m. on July 8, 2006.

IN WITNESS WHEREOF, Optionor and Optionee have set their hands the date aforesaid.

David D. Jones   Donald S. Reed
Optionor   Optionee

Robert B. Big   Sally M. Little
Witness   Witness

Copyright Thomas J. Lucier 2005. To customize this document, download it to your hard drive from Thomas J. Lucier's web site at www.thomaslucier.com/optionforms.html. The document can then be opened, edited, and printed using Microsoft Word or another popular word processing application.

CHAPTER 18

How to Clean Up a Property under Option to Maximize Its Curb Appeal and Resale Value

It always amazes me how a professionally applied industrial-strength cleaning can dramatically improve any property's appearance. And that is exactly why I told you in Chapter 14 to always include a clause in your option agreement that gives you the right to enter and clean the property during the option period. You must give a property under option an old-fashioned industrial-strength cleaning to:

1. Make the property more visible and accessible to prospective buyers passing by.
2. Keep vandals, arsonists, homeless squatters, and drug addicts from gaining easy access to the property.
3. Maximize the property's curb appeal.
4. Increase the property's resale value.

If you followed my advice in Chapter 13, you should have negotiated a $500 cleaning credit, which the owner deducted from the option fee. The cleaning credit is to help investors defray property cleanup costs. And depending on the property's size and condition, most of my cleanups run from $500 to $1,200. For example, it usually costs me right around $500 to have a vacant three-bedroom, two-bathroom, single-family house cleaned up. This includes trash removal, lawn mowing, tree trimming, and pressure washing. I spend between $500 and $1,200 for an industrial-strength cleaning on a vacant piece of commercial property. I use a father and son team, who specialize in clearing lots, hauling trash, pressure washing, and making buildings secure. My guys are experienced professionals with state-of-the-art equipment, who work fast and charge reasonable rates. But most importantly, they do the job right the first time and I do not have to babysit them.

Don't Confuse an Industrial Cleaning with an Extreme Property Makeover

There is a world of difference between giving a property an industrial-strength cleaning and doing an extreme makeover like the ones shown on TV, where they take a building apart and put it back together. An industrial-strength cleaning is nothing more than a very thorough cleaning, which dramatically improves a property's curb appeal by:

1. Removing all of the trash from the building and grounds.
2. Putting the building and grounds in a broom- and rake-clean condition.
3. Cutting and removing all of the overgrown brush, grass, and weeds from the grounds.
4. Trimming shrubs and trees.
5. Pressure washing all exterior walls to remove grime, mildew, mold, graffiti, and peeling paint.
6. Pressure washing concrete walkways to remove grime, mold, grease, and oil.

Whatever you do, please do not do like a rookie option investor in Dallas, Texas, who got carried away during a property cleanup and had new carpet installed in a house he had under a three-month option. I learned about this big-time blunder when the investor sent me an e-mail, lamenting about how he lost $4,500 on his first option deal. As I told him in my reply, his first mistake was in paying $2,000 for a three-month option with no right to extend the option period. And then he compounded his mistake by having $2,500 worth of carpet installed in a house he did not own. The option expired before he was able to find a buyer and he was out $4,500, with nothing to show for the time, effort, and money he had spent on the property.

How to Complete a Fast Property Cleanup on Schedule and within Budget

Once a property is put under option, time is money and you cannot afford to dilly-dally around with the cleanup. And the trick to completing a fast property cleanup on schedule and within budget is in knowing how to:

1. *Plan:* Develop a cleanup plan based on the property's appearance and information that was derived about the property's physical condition during your pre-buy inspection of the property.

2. *Budget:* Calculate a budget by using a bottom-line mentality, which is based on exactly what needs to be done to maximize the property's visibility, accessibility, curb appeal, and resale value and nothing more. In other words, when you calculate your cleanup budget, use the bare minimum amount of money necessary to obtain the maximum return on every dollar spent cleaning up the property.

3. *Schedule:* I use what is referred to in the military as *backward planning* to establish a cleaning schedule timetable. I do this by calculating a realistic completion date, which is based on a six-day workweek and takes possible unforeseen problems and local weather conditions into consideration. Once I have established my property cleanup completion date, which for me is never more than six days from the start date, I establish a work schedule for each phase of the cleanup.

4. *Hire:* If you do not have the knowledge, experience, time, or desire to do a professional cleaning job, hire competent professionals to do it for you.

5. *Supervise:* If you do not have the knowledge and time to supervise the cleanup yourself, hire a competent professional to do it for you.

How to Clean Up and Secure a Vacant Property under Option

First things first: Always start cleaning a vacant property from the front sidewalk and work your way to the rear property line. You should always start your cleanup from the front sidewalk to enhance the property's curb appeal and make it more visible and enticing to prospective buyers passing by. Here is a sequential listing of how you should clean up and secure a vacant property:

1. Cut and remove overgrown brush, grass, and weeds.
2. Trim trees and shrubs and remove cut branches.
3. Put the grounds in a rake-clean condition and remove all trash and debris.
4. Pressure wash asphalt shingle and tile roofs.
5. Pressure wash exterior walls.
6. Pressure wash concrete walkways.
7. Put the interior of the building in a broom-clean condition and remove all trash and debris.

8. Secure all broken door and window openings with half-inch CDX plywood.

9. Lock the main entry door with a heavy-duty commercial grade Master hasp lock and keyed high-security Master padlock.

10. Attach a 4- by 8-foot "for sale" sign to the exterior building wall facing traffic, which has your telephone number and e-mail address so you can be contacted in case of an emergency.

How to Find Competent Professionals to Clean Up Your Properties

If you do not have the time or desire to clean up properties yourself or you cringe at the thought of getting your hands dirty or a blister on your little pinkie finger, I suggest that you hire out your property cleanups to professionals. The best source of competent cleaning professionals that I have been able to find is retired construction workers. Here in Florida, there are a lot of retired construction workers who are always looking for part-time employment. And for the most part, these guys do top-quality work at fair prices, which are a fraction of what a cleaning contractor would charge. In addition to hiring retired construction workers, you can visit construction job sites and ask laborers if they are interested in what is commonly called side work. Once you find laborers who want to work for you, ask them to provide references from people they have done work for in the past.

How to Avoid Being Ripped Off by Unscrupulous Cleaning Contractors

Keep in mind that a little investigative work on your part can help you avoid becoming the next victim of some fly-by-night huckster posing as Mr. or Ms. Clean. Here are five ways that you can avoid being ripped off by an unscrupulous cleaning contractor:

1. Require that you be given a copy of the contractor's general liability insurance certificate, and then contact the insurer listed on the certificate to verify that the policy is valid and in effect.

2. Contact your local Better Business Bureau to see if there is a history of complaints against the contractor.

3. Require that you be given at least three verifiable customer references, and contact each one of the references and ask if they would hire the contractor again.

4. Require written estimates for all cleaning jobs.

5. Require that everyone who provides labor on your job sign your state's version of a release of lien upon final payment.

What You Need to Know about Your State's Construction Lien Law

You need to know that under most state construction lien laws, anyone who provides a service, labor, or materials for the improvement of real property has a right to file a lien against the property's title for non-payment. Furthermore, if you do pay a contractor for a job and the contractor fails to pay the subcontractors who supplied the labor and the materials suppliers, you are still financially responsible for paying them, even though you have paid the contractor in full. In other words, you could end up paying for a job twice if you do not have legal proof that everyone was paid in full. The only way to avoid having this happen to you is to require that everyone who supplies services, labor, and materials on your property cleanup sign your state's version of a release of lien upon final payment. This way, you will have legal proof that everyone connected to your property cleanup has been paid in full.

Best to Rent a Dumpster for Large Cleanups

The very first thing that you should do when cleaning up a property is to have all of the loose trash and debris swept and raked up and put into heavy-duty 42-gallon plastic bags. And then have the ends of the bags tied off with tie wire so that the trash does not spill out when the bags are picked up. I use Husky Contractor Clean-Up Bags, which are available at Home Depot and Lowe's stores nationwide. But when you have a large amount of trash and debris that needs to be removed from a property, it may be less expensive to rent an open-top, roll-off solid waste container, better known as a dumpster. Dumpsters are available in sizes ranging from 10 to 40 cubic yards. For example, here in Tampa, I can rent a 20-cubic yard container for seven days for $289, which includes pickup and delivery. But I have to pay an additional $45 per ton when the container is hauled off. And when full, most 20-foot containers weigh between 3 and 4 tons. I ended up paying $469 for the last 20-cubic yard container I rented. Please note that most companies do not allow dirt, concrete, roofing materials, or appliances to be placed in their containers. You can log on to the following web sites to obtain information about dumpster rates and availability in your area:

Waste Management: www.wm.com

Dumpsters USA: www.dumpstersusa.com

Pressure Washing Pays the Highest Return of Any Type of Cleaning

At one time I owned a commercial pressure washing company in Tampa, so I know from firsthand experience how a properly applied pressure washing job can dramatically change the appearance of any building, asphalt shingle and tile roof, and flat surfaces, such as concrete sidewalks and driveway. The two keys to a great-looking pressure-washing job are state-of-the-art equipment and properly formulated cleaning chemicals. A professional pressure washer will have the right pieces of equipment to clean all types of washable surfaces and will use chemicals specially formulated to remove soot, scum, mold, grease, grime, mildew, and rust from all types of washable surfaces. And believe me, a pressure washing machine with an 18 horsepower engine, operating at 3,500 pounds per square inch of pressure (PSI), with a water flow rate of 3.5 gallons per minute (GPM), is capable of cleaning any washable surface to the point where it looks brand, spanking new. For example, I have been able to pressure wash stucco and concrete block walls coated with layers of grime, soot, mold, and mildew that had accumulated over the years and make them look like they were just built. And I have also been able to clean asphalt shingle and tile roofs that were filthy from mold and mildew and make them look like new, without damaging any shingles or tiles. I have had the same results cleaning concrete surfaces, too. Trust me, after you have had a building cleaned by a professional pressure washing service, you will be absolutely amazed at the dramatic difference it makes to the building's appearance!

Make the Property Secure from Vandals, Arsonists, and Homeless Squatters

Vacant properties act as a magnet for vandals, arsonists, homeless squatters, and drug addicts. And the last thing you want to happen when showing a property is for the prospective buyer to be spooked by some crack addict passed out cold on the floor. The easiest, quickest, and least expensive way to stop anyone from gaining easy access to a property is to remove or trim all of the trees, shrubs, and plants around door and window openings and make the openings secure. I put half-inch CDX plywood over broken window and door openings the same way that property preservation services board up vacant properties for lenders and insurance companies. This way, law enforcement officers will be able to see when someone is attempting to break into a property in broad daylight. I install a heavy-duty commercial grade Master hasp lock on the main entry door and lock it with the same high-security keyed Master padlock that is used on military installations.

Always Conduct a Walk-Through Inspection before Making Final Payments

Before you shell out any of your hard-earned cash and make any final payments to cleaning contractors, first do a walk-through inspection of the property to determine if all work has been satisfactorily completed. When doing your walk-through inspection, make a list of any discrepancies you find, and give it to the contractor to correct. In doing this, be fair and realistic, but do not let anyone take unfair advantage of you. When making your final payments, be certain you get a release of lien form signed by the contractor, which states that he or she has been paid in full for all of the labor and materials used on your property cleanup.

Best to Keep Track of Your Property Cleanup Expenses on a Daily Basis

The best way to avoid getting carried away during a property cleanup and end up with a huge cost overrun on the job is to keep track of your cleanup costs on a daily basis. And the easiest way to do this is by maintaining a daily cleanup cost worksheet like the sample on page 191 to record both your material and labor costs.

FORM 18.1   Sample Daily Cleanup Cost Worksheet

Date	Material Costs	Labor Costs	Miscellaneous	Total Cost

CHAPTER 19

How to Package, Market, and Resell Your Real Estate Options for Maximum Profit

Throughout the course of this book, I have given you detailed, step-by-step instructions on how to use real estate options to control undervalued properties with immediate resale profit potential. In this business, you make your profit upfront when you buy low-cost options on properties that are priced well below market value. But you do not get paid until you turn around and resell the option for a profit. And getting paid is what this chapter is all about! It should not take a rocket scientist to understand that there is a direct correlation between how well a property is marketed and how fast an option sells. If you do not get anything else from this chapter, please get this: Market the property, not the real estate option. Never lose sight of the fact that what you are really selling is not the real estate option agreement itself, but rather the property under option. The fact is, I have never advertised a real estate option per se; instead, I have always advertised the property under option. The trick to quickly reselling your options is to target your marketing toward prospective buyers of the type of property under option. For example, I recently resold an option on a run-down, rail-front bulk warehouse, which had been used to store bags of building materials, such as cement, stucco, sand, and pre-mixed concrete. For your information, the term *rail-front* refers to properties accessible by rail. To find prospective buyers for a rail-front warehouse located in Tampa, Florida, I went online and did Google searches for construction-related trade associations, building materials manufacturers, and distributors. And from my search results, I was able to compile a listing of 30 prospective buyers. I e-mailed each prospect a detailed property fact sheet, which included a picture of the property facing the railroad tracks. Two months later, I ended up reselling my option to a distributor of silica sand, which is used in sandblasting. I was able to resell my option on a rail-front bulk warehouse because I focused my marketing on prospective buyers who would have a need for that particular type of property. In this chapter, I give you the lowdown on exactly how to:

1. Calculate the resale value of real estate options.
2. Package properties under option to highlight their best features.
3. Market properties under option so you can sell your option agreements for maximum profit.
4. Assign or sell option agreements to third parties so you can make money in real estate without ever actually buying any property.

How to Calculate the Resale Price for a Real Estate Option

The first step in the process of reselling a real estate option is to calculate its resale value. There is an old adage in real estate sales, which goes something like this: "Getting greedy will get you needy." Please keep this sage advice in mind when you are pricing your options for resale. In other words, do not try to suck every last dime out of the deal. Instead, price your real estate options so there is enough profit potential to entice prospective buyers. I always try to sell my real estate options for at least 10 percent of the property's market value. For example, on a property with a fair market value of $250,000 that I have an option to buy for $190,000, I would price my option at $30,000. This way, I would be fairly compensated for the time and effort that it took me to get the property under option. And whoever buys my option would still be able to buy the property for $30,000 below market value when he or she exercises the option. You can use the same step-by-step instructions that I outlined in Chapter 12 to estimate a property's market value. When calculating the resale price of a real estate option, do not forget to include the cost of:

1. Searching for the property.
2. Buying the real estate option.
3. Putting the property in a marketable condition.
4. Marketing the property.
5. Your time spent on the transaction.

Package Properties to Fully Highlight Their Best Features and Future Potential

You do not need to be a rocket scientist to be able to quickly figure out that how much you are able to sell your real estate options for is tied directly to how well you are able to package the properties you own options on. *Packaging a property* means to present the property to prospective buyers in a way that fully highlights its best features and future potential uses. As part of my marketing plan, I compile a comprehensive property information sheet, which lists the following features about any property that I have under option:

1. The year the property was built, along with the type of construction and architectural style.
2. The property's geographical location, to include any special features or benefits about the area.
3. A brief description of the building's interior, to include the square footage and geometrical shape of the building, spacing between interior support columns, ceiling and overhead door heights, type of heating and cooling system, and the size and shape of the lot.
4. Nearby sources of available transportation, to include rail, highway, airport, and port facilities.

And when I want to highlight a property's potential future uses, I make a listing of every conceivable way in which the property could be used. To illustrate, I once owned a one-year option on a vacant gasoline station, which was located on a busy intersection in North Tampa. The property belonged to a regional chain, which had scaled back on the size of its operation in Tampa Bay. The downside to the property was that all of the underground storage tanks leaked like a sieve and had to be replaced before the property could be used again as a gas station. However, the property's upside was that it could still be put to other uses. So I proceeded to market the property for future use as a:

1. Quick oil change and lube shop.
2. Auto repair shop.
3. Auto upholstery shop.
4. Used car lot.
5. Motorcycle repair shop.

Three months later, I resold my option to a "Buy here; pay here" used car lot operator, who eventually went bankrupt and never exercised its option. Today, five years later, it is the site of a Walgreens Drugstore.

How to Overcome the "Fear Factor" That Some Prospective Buyers May Have

Once you get into this business, you will very quickly realize that the biggest fear that every option buyer has is that somehow, the optionor will renege on his or her option agreement by refusing to sell the property after the option has been exercised. The only way that I know to overcome this fear factor is to follow my advice in Chapter 17 and have all of the property title transfer documents signed by the optionor and held in escrow by your real estate attorney or title or escrow agent during the option period. Please believe me when I tell you that it so much easier to sell a real estate option agreement when you can show prospective buyers signed and notarized copies of all the property title transfer documents that are needed to close on the purchase of the property under option. For example, when I assign or sell a real estate option to a third party, I prepare an option assignment package, which I give to the assignee or buyer, that includes copies of the following documents:

1. Joint escrow instructions.
2. Real estate option agreement.
3. Title search report.
4. Title insurance policy insuring the real estate option.
5. Addendum real estate purchase agreement stamped "Copy only."
6. Warranty or grant deed stamped "Copy only."
7. Buyer's HUD 1 Settlement Statement.

Five Best Methods to Market Properties That You Own Real Estate Options On

I have found the following five methods to be the most effective ways to market properties under option to potential buyers:

1. Property for sale web pages.
2. Property for sale ads online.
3. Property e-mail fact sheets.
4. Property for sale signs.
5. Classified property for sale ads.

How to Use the Internet to Market Your Properties Globally

The key to quickly reselling your real estate options is to market properties under option to the largest possible number of prospective buyers. In today's wired world, this includes the global audience of potential buyers, which are available online via the World Wide Web. And in spite of what some foreigners may think about our political leaders, American real estate still attracts investors from around the globe. For example, here in Central Florida, real estate investors from the United Kingdom, Germany, the Netherlands, Canada, and Spain are continually investing in residential and commercial real estate. The main reason I like European investors so much is that they are generally cash buyers, who are ready, willing, and financially able to close a deal without first having to play the mortgage loan disqualification game with lenders in order to finance the purchase. I once sold an option that I had on a small warehouse to a German, who exported German Christmas decorations to the Southeast United States. This guy loved the Tampa Bay area, and he had found out about the property by doing a Google search using the term, "Tampa warehouses for sale." As far as I am concerned, it is absolutely imperative that you use the Internet to tap into the global real estate marketplace and expose your properties to prospective buyers worldwide, by using:

1. Property for sale web pages.
2. Property for sale ads online.
3. Property e-mail fact sheets.

Create a Property for Sale Web Page to Advertise Your Properties Online

If you already have a web site, all you will have to do is to create a property for sale web page to advertise your properties for sale online. To see an example of a property for sale web page, log on to my web site, www.homeequitiescorp.com, and click on the Property for Sale button. I recommend that you include the following information on your property for sale web page:

1. Interior and exterior photographs of the property.
2. Property location map.
3. Driving directions to the property.

4. Property site plan.

5. Property features.

6. Property's sale price and terms.

7. Information on how to set up an appointment to view the property.

Also, make certain that you include a buyer e-mail notification form on your web page. One of the most efficient ways to compile a listing of prospective buyers is to have visitors to your web site complete a buyer e-mail notification form so that they can submit their name and e-mail address in order to be notified by e-mail when you have a property for sale. When notifying prospective buyers via e-mail about a property that you own a real estate option on, send them an e-mail property fact sheet that includes the following information:

1. Property address.

2. Description of the property.

3. Estimate of the property's current market value.

4. Sale price and terms of the property.

5. Real estate option sale price.

6. Location map of the property.

7. Site plan of the property.

8. Directions to the property.

Use URL Forwarding for Property for Sale Domain Names

In Chapter 9, I explained how uniform resource locator (URL) forwarding works for a property wanted domain name. The same principle applies when using URL forwarding for a property for sale domain name. For example, I own the domain name, www.tampapropertyforsale.com, which is forwarded to the Property for Sale web page on the Home Equities Corp web site at www.homeequitiescorp.com. This way, whenever the domain name www.tampapropertyforsale.com is typed into an Internet browser or search engine, it is automatically forwarded to the Home Equities Corp Property for Sale web page.

Sources of Online Mapping Services

The following is a listing of web sites that provide online location maps and driving directions, which you can use on your property for sale web page:

MapQuest: www.mapquest.com

MapBlast: www.mapblast.com

Maptech: www.mapserver.maptech.com

Expedia: www.expedia.com

Topozone: www.tpozone.com

Yahoo Maps: www.maps.yahoo.com

Maps: www.maps.com

Advertise Your Properties for Sale Online

The following is a listing of web sites where you can advertise your properties online:

Real Buyer: www.realbuyer.net

Biz Trader: www.biztrader.com

REBUZ: www.rebuz.com

Loopnet: www.loopnet.com

Post Your Property: www.postyourproperty.com

Apartments for Sale: www.apartmentsales.com

Land Net: www.land.net

Realty Investor: www.realtyinvestor.com

Dealmakers Commercial Property Forum: commercial-realestate@dealmakers .net

Dealmakers Investment Property Forum: Investment-realestate@dealmakers .net

Always Place a Professional-Looking "For Sale" Sign on the Property

Another marketing tool that you always want to use to advertise your property is a professional-looking "for sale" sign placed in a strategic location on the property. The sign by itself may not sell the property, but it will let passersby know that the property is for sale. I use 4-foot by 4-foot signs, which are made from ¾-inch marine grade plywood and attached to 4-inch by 4-inch by 8-foot pressure-treated posts. My signs have a white background, and the numbers and letters are painted in red and black by a professional sign painter. My signs are made out of marine-grade plywood because it is very durable and does not delaminate after it becomes wet. All of my signs have my web site address, e-mail address, and telephone number prominently displayed like the following sample sign:

Property for Sale

www.tampapropertyforsale.com

Sales@tampapropertyforsale.com

Call (813) 237-6267 Today!

Place Classified Ads in Local Newspapers

In addition to using property for sale web pages, online advertising, e-mail property fact sheets, and "for sale" signs to market your properties, I recommend that you place classified ads like the following sample in local daily and weekly newspapers, with your web site address, e-mail address, and telephone number in the body of the ad. Notice that the information in the ad is exactly the same as the sign.

Property for Sale

www.tampapropertyforsale.com

Sales@tampapropertyforsale.com

Call (813) 237-6267 Today!

How to Sell Your Real Estate Option Agreements

When you sell or assign a real estate option agreement, you transfer the ownership of the real estate option by doing what is called an *assignment of real estate option agreement*. To do this, you, as the assignor, and the buyer, as the assignee, both sign an assignment of real estate option agreement, like the sample on page 200, in

---

FORM 19.1   Sample Assignment of Real Estate Option Agreement

---

This agreement made this tenth day of September 2005 between Donald S. Reed, hereinafter known as the Assignor, and James R. Black, hereinafter known as the Assignee. Assignor and Assignee hereby agree as follows:

In return for the consideration set forth in this agreement, Assignor hereby assigns, sells, and transfers all of Assignor's rights and interests under the attached agreement entitled Real Estate Option Agreement dated July 9, 2004, known hereinafter as the "Agreement," executed by David D. Jones as Optionor, and by Assignor Donald S. Reed, as Optionee, for the real estate option to purchase said property known as: 45735 Hillsborough Avenue, Tampa, Florida 33603, and legally described as: Lots 47, 48 and 49 of Carter's subdivision according to map or plat thereof as recorded in plat book 69, page 89, of the public records of Hillsborough County, Florida.

By accepting this assignment, Assignee agrees to undertake and perform any obligations imposed on Assignor as Optionee under the aforementioned Agreement. Assignee accepts this assignment subject to all terms and conditions contained in the Agreement or imposed by law. A copy of the Agreement is attached hereto and incorporated herein as if fully set forth herein.

It is hereby agreed that it is the sole responsibility of Assignee to comply with the terms of the Agreement, and it is the sole responsibility of Assignee to seek legal or other relief in the event that the agreement is not performed as a result of the act or omission of any other party to the Agreement.

In return for the rights and interests assigned by Assignor, Assignee hereby agrees to pay Assignor the sum of fifteen thousand dollars ($15,000), payable in United States currency, by cashier's check, drawn on a local bank.

Assignee shall, upon signing this Agreement, deposit said sum with Assignor. All provisions of this Agreement shall extend to, bind, and inure to the benefit of heirs, executors, personal representatives, successors, and assigns of Assignor and Assignee.

IN WITNESS WHEREOF, Assignor and Assignee have set their hands the date aforesaid.

Donald S. Reed   James R. Black
Assignor   Assignee

Robert B. Big   Sally M. Little
Witness   Witness

Copyright Thomas J. Lucier 2005. To customize this document, download it to your hard drive from Thomas J. Lucier's web site at www.thomaslucier.com/optionforms.html. The document can then be opened, edited, and printed using Microsoft Word or another popular word processing application.

the presence of a notary public, in which you assign or sell all of your rights and interests in the real estate option agreement to the buyer.

Notify the Optionor That You Have Assigned Your Real Estate Option Agreement

Once you have assigned or sold your real estate option agreement, you must notify the optionor of the assignment by sending a notice of assignment of real estate option agreement like the following sample notice. Send your letter by U.S. Postal Service Certified Mail, return receipt requested, so that you have verifiable proof it was received. Also, send a copy to the attorney or escrow or title agent holding the property title transfer documents in escrow.

FORM 19.2   Sample Notice of Assignment of Real Estate Option Agreement

---

September 10, 2005

Mr. David D. Jones
5300 West Oklahoma Avenue
Tampa, FL 33629

Dear Mr. Jones:

Please take notice that on this tenth day of September 2005, I have assigned all of my rights and interest in that certain Real Estate Option Agreement, executed by you as Optionor, to me, as Optionee, on July 9, 2005, to Robert D. Johnson, whose post office mailing address is 4709 Swan Avenue, Tampa, FL 33606.

A copy of the Assignment of Real Estate Option Agreement is attached to this letter of notification.

Sincerely,

Donald S. Reed

Attachment: Assignment of Real Estate Option Agreement

Copyright Thomas J. Lucier 2005. To customize this document, download it to your hard drive from Thomas J. Lucier's web site at www.thomaslucier.com/optionforms.html. The document can then be opened, edited, and printed using Microsoft Word or another popular word processing application.

How Income from the Sale of Real Estate Options is Treated for Tax Purposes

Income earned from the sale of real estate options is taxed at the same rate as ordinary earned income. And for tax purposes, the IRS will consider you to be a real estate dealer versus an investor because you are buying options with the intent to resell and not as an investment. Real estate options are covered in Section 1234 of the Internal Revenue Code, which is provided for your convenience:

Internal Revenue Code, Section 1234, Options to Buy or Sell

1234(a)(1) GENERAL RULE.—Gain or loss attributable to the sale or exchange of, or loss attributable to failure to exercise, an option to buy or sell property shall be considered gain or loss from the sale or exchange of property which has the same character as the property to which the option relates has in the hands of the taxpayer (or would have in the hands of the taxpayer if acquired by him).

1234(a)(2) SPECIAL RULE FOR LOSS ATTRIBUTABLE TO FAILURE TO EXERCISE OPTION.—For purposes of paragraph (1), if loss is attributable to failure to exercise an option, the option shall be deemed to have been sold or exchanged on the day it expired.

1234(a)(3) NONAPPLICATION OF SUBSECTION.—This subsection shall not apply to—

1234(a)(3)(A) an option which constitutes property described in paragraph (1) of section 1221(a)

1234(a)(3)(B) in the case of gain attributable to the sale or exchange of an option, any income derived in connection with such option which, without regard to this subsection, is treated as other than gain from the sale or exchange of a capital asset; and

1234(a)(3)(C) a loss attributable to failure to exercise an option described in section 1233(c).

1234(b) TREATMENT OF GRANTOR OF OPTION IN THE CASE OF STOCK, SECURITIES, OR COMMODITIES.—

1234(b)(1) GENERAL RULE.—In the case of the grantor of the option, gain or loss from any closing transaction with respect to, and gain on lapse of, an option in property shall be treated as a gain or loss from the sale or exchange of a capital asset held not more than 1 year.

1234(b)(2) DEFINITIONS.—For purposes of this subsection—

1234(b)(2)(A) CLOSING TRANSACTION.—The term "closing transaction" means any termination of the taxpayer's obligation under an option in property other than through the exercise or lapse of the option.

1234(b)(2)(B) PROPERTY.—The term "property" means stocks and securities (including stocks and securities dealt with on a "when issued" basis), commodities, and commodity futures.

1234(b)(3) NONAPPLICATION OF SUBSECTION.—This subsection shall not apply to any option granted in the ordinary course of the taxpayer's trade or business of granting options.

1234(c) TREATMENT OF OPTIONS ON

1234(c)(1)

1234(c)(2) TREATMENT OF CASH SETTLEMENT OPTIONS.

1234(c)(2)(A) IN GENERAL.—For purposes of subsections (a) and (b), a cash settlement option shall be treated as an option to buy or sell property.

1234(c)(2)(B) CASH SETTLEMENT OPTION.—For purposes of subparagraph (A), the term "cash settlement option" means any option which on exercise settles in (or could be settled in) cash or property other than the underlying property.

Internal Revenue Service
Publications Are Available Online

IRS forms and publications are available online in PDF format at the following web page: www.irs.gov/formspubs/index.html.

Use the U.S. Master Tax Guide as
Your Tax Reference Guide

I highly recommend that you use the *U.S. Master Tax Guide* as your tax reference guide. It is published annually by the Commerce Clearinghouse and available at the following web site: http://tax.cchgroup.com.

Best to Hire a Properly Licensed Professional to Prepare Your Tax Returns

Unless you are a certified public accountant, board-certified tax attorney, or an enrolled agent, you should hire a tax professional who is licensed to represent taxpayers before all administrative levels of the IRS to prepare your tax returns. And yes, I am very well aware of all of the inexpensive off-the-shelf tax preparation software programs that are available today. However, here is an excellent reason I very strongly recommend that real estate investors never, ever use any of these software programs to prepare their tax returns: Who from the tax preparation software conglomerate is going to represent you in front of the IRS when you're audited because there was an unreported glitch in their software program that flubbed up your tax return? Answer: Absolutely no one! That is because you are on your own when you rely on XYZ tax preparation software to prepare your tax return. This is not the case when you hire a properly licensed tax professional to prepare your tax returns. For example, I have used the same enrolled agent to prepare my state and federal tax returns since 1985, and I have never had a single tax return questioned by anyone. However, the main reason I continue to use the same tax professional is that part of the tax preparation service is free representation in front of the IRS—without my having to be present—if there are ever any questions about the return or in the event of an audit. It's akin to having a free IRS audit insurance policy!

CHAPTER 20

How to Exercise Your Option and Buy the Property

In this business, there will be times when you have a property under option that you want to buy and hold on to. And when a so-called keeper property comes along, you will need to know how to exercise your option and actually buy the property. To avoid the usual confusion and aggravation, which are a part of most real estate closings, I recommend that you follow my advice in Chapter 17 and always use a board-certified real estate attorney to close all of your real estate transactions. The keys to a flawless closing are planning, organization, and attention to details. Close may be good enough for hand grenades and horseshoes, but a close-enough-for-government-work attitude can lead to financially fatal mistakes when closing on the purchase of a property under option. In this final chapter of the book, I give you all of the nitty-gritty details that you need to know in order to avoid the common closing pitfalls that plague most novice option investors. As far as I am concerned, the worst fate that can befall any option investor is to be one step away from pay dirt and then have everything blow up at the closing table because of a screw-up that should have been caught and corrected in time to save the deal, but it was not because someone involved in the closing was asleep at the switch. And the hapless investor was clueless until after the damage was done, and it was too late to do anything about it. So please trust me when I tell you that the only way that you are going to be able to avoid being treated like a mushroom—fed a lot of bullspit and kept in the dark—at the closing table is to take a hands-on approach when you exercise your option and buy the property.

How to Exercise Your Real Estate Option

First things first: Once you decide to purchase a property under option, you must exercise your real estate option. And you can do this by sending the optionor an exercise of real estate option notification letter like the sample on page 207. I recommend that you send your letter by U.S. Postal Service Certified Mail, return receipt requested, so you have verifiable proof that it was received by the optionor. Also, send a copy of the notification letter to the attorney or escrow or title agent holding all of the property title transfer documents in escrow.

How to Purchase a Property under Option

After you have exercised your real estate option, you must purchase the property under option or assign the agreement to a third party. And if you followed my advice in Chapter 16, you should already have a purchase agreement signed by the optionor in escrow. Your purchase agreement should have been included as an addendum to your option agreement. If you did not have the optionor sign a separate purchase agreement, you should have included a clause in your option agreement stating that it would automatically ripen into a purchase agreement once the option was exercised. Either way, you and the optionor should have already worked out exactly how the sale of the property is going to take place.

Fourteen Key Provisions That Must Be Included in Your Purchase Agreement

Please, whatever you do, do not, I repeat, do not use the same real estate purchase agreements that are used by real estate licensees in your state to document the purchase of a property under option. I say this because virtually all of the real estate agreements used by real estate licensees are written to protect the licensees' sales commissions and the legal rights and interests of the sellers who have listed their property through real estate brokers. In addition to not being buyer-friendly, these purchase and sale agreements are also not investor-friendly, as they are geared toward traditional run-of-the-mill real estate transactions with conventional terms. Instead, I recommend that you hire a board-certified real estate attorney to prepare a purchase agreement that protects your rights and interests as a buyer. And make certain that the following 14 key provisions are included in your purchase agreement to clearly define the terms and conditions of the agreement and the rights and responsibilities of both the buyer and the seller:

1. *Parties to the agreement:* Designate all parties to the purchase agreement as buyer and seller to include their legal status as to whether they are a single

FORM 20.1   Sample Exercise of Real Estate Option Notification Letter

September 10, 2005

Mr. David D. Jones
5300 West Oklahoma Avenue
Tampa, FL 33629

Dear Mr. Jones:

Please take notice that on this tenth day of September 2005, I have elected to exercise the real estate option given by you to me, on July 9, 2005 to purchase the property therein described, pursuant to the terms and conditions of our Real Estate Option Agreement and Real Estate Purchase Agreement held in escrow by Mr. John B. Good, attorney at law, whose law office is located at 6907 Charleston Court, Tampa, Florida 33607.

Sincerely,

Donald S. Reed

individual, husband and wife, or a business entity such as a corporation or limited liability company.

2. *Earnest money deposit:* State that the option fee shall be used as the earnest money deposit and applied toward the down payment.

3. *Legal description of property:* Use the exact legal description that is written on the recorded deed of the property in the purchase agreement.

4. *Purchase price:* State that the firm purchase price of the property is the same as the purchase price listed in the option agreement.

5. *Terms of purchase:* Specify exactly how the purchase of the property is going to be financed.

6. *Marketable title:* Specify that the buyer must be able to obtain an owner's title insurance policy commitment letter from a title insurer in order to close on the purchase of the property.

7. *Assignment of the purchase agreement:* Include a clause that the buyer has the right to assign or sell the purchase agreement to a third party.

8. *Default by buyer:* Specify that the earnest money paid is the sole and exclusive remedy in the event that the buyer or buyer's assigns fail to close on the purchase of the property.

9. *Default by seller:* State that the buyer or buyer's assigns shall have the right of specific performance in the event the seller defaults on the agreement by refusing to sell the property.

10. *Eminent domain:* Specify that the buyer or buyer's assign shall be entitled to a full refund of the earnest money deposit paid, plus any accrued interest, in the event the property is condemned by eminent domain prior to the closing date.

11. *Buyer's right of entry:* State that the buyer or the buyer's assigns have the right, upon giving the owner 24 hours' notice, to enter the property and inspect, repair, market, and show it to third parties prior to the closing date.

12. *Risk of loss:* Specify that the buyer or buyer's assigns are entitled to a full refund of the earnest money deposit paid, plus accrued interest, in the event the property is damaged or destroyed by fire, storm, or earthquake prior to the closing date.

13. *Right to examine records:* State that the buyer or buyer's assigns have the right to examine all of the financial and tax records associated with the property prior to the closing date.

14. *Seller must vacate property:* Require that the seller completely vacate the property and grounds prior to the closing date.

Three Contingency Clauses That Must Be Included in Your Purchase Agreement

When it comes to protecting your position as buyer in a real estate transaction, you must make certain to cover yourself in case unexpected problems arise when it is time to close the deal. And this is especially true when buying a property that has been under option for six months to a year. This is why I highly recommend that you include the following three contingency clauses in your purchase agreement:

1. *Buyer must approve of the property's title status and marketability before this transaction can be closed.* Include this clause in the event there have been liens or lawsuits filed against the property's title or owner since the option was purchased that adversely affect the property's marketability.

2. *Buyer must approve of the status of the property's existing loans before this transaction can be closed.* This clause must be included in case any of the property's loans are in foreclosure.

3. *Seller must completely vacate the property and grounds before this transaction can be closed.* This clause protects the buyer from getting stuck with an obstinate property owner or a hostile tenant who refuses to peaceably leave the property after the sale has closed and the property's title has been transferred to the new owner.

On my third option deal, I got the shock of my young career when I exercised my option and a title search revealed that the property under option was in the throes of foreclosure and just two weeks away from being sold on the Hillsborough County Courthouse steps. Come to find out, the property owners were in the middle of a nasty divorce, and they had stopped making mortgage payments months ago. I tried to get them to sell me their equity so that I could cure the loan default, reinstate the mortgage, and stop the foreclosure action, but they could not agree on a price. And two weeks later the loan was foreclosed on, and my $2,000 option fee/earnest money deposit was wiped out in the process. I thought about filing a lawsuit against them in small claims court to try to recover my earnest money deposit, but I found out from reliable sources that they were flat broke and did not have two quarters to rub together. I could not get mad at myself because I had no way of knowing they were going to be getting a divorce six months from when we all signed the option agreement. At that time, they were acting very lovey-dovey, like everything in their life was just hunky-dory.

I have included the sample real estate purchase agreement on pages 210–211 for instructional and informational purposes only. Please do not use this agreement to purchase property in your state without first consulting with a board-certified real estate attorney to make certain that it meets all of your state's real estate contract standards.

What You Need to Know about the
Real Estate Settlement Procedures Act

The Real Estate Settlement Procedures Act, better known as RESPA, is a federal consumer statute that was enacted into law in 1974 to protect the property-buying public from being ripped off by the real estate industry, which consists of title insurers, escrow companies, mortgage and deed of trust lenders, mortgage brokers, real estate agents, and attorneys who perform real estate settlements or closings. HUD is responsible for enforcing RESPA nationwide. And according to HUD, the

---

FORM 20.2   Sample Real Estate Purchase Agreement

This Agreement is made this ninth day of July 2005 between Donald S. Reed, a single man, known hereinafter as the Buyer, and Robert D. Johnson, a single man, known hereinafter as the Seller. Seller agrees to convey, transfer, assign, sell, and deliver to Buyer or assigns all of Seller's rights, title, and interest in and to the following property known as: 45735 Hillsborough Avenue, Tampa, Florida 33603, and legally described as: Lots 47, 48, and 49 of Carters subdivision according to map or plat thereof as recorded in plat book 69, page 89, of the public record of Hillsborough County, Florida, which Seller agree to sell to Buyer and Buyer or assigns agrees to buy from Seller.

Purchase Price $350,000.00

Method of Payment:

Real estate option consideration paid in the amount of $5,000.00

Buyer to assume that first mortgage loan with an approximate principal
balance of $295,000.00

and dated August 28, 1997, and executed by Robert J. Johnson, as mortgagor, to Bank of America, as mortgagee, in the original amount of three-hundred and five thousand dollars ($305,000), which mortgage was duly recorded in the office of the Clerk of the Circuit Court of Hillsborough County, State of Florida, in book 790346, on page 45905, of the public records of Hillsborough County, Florida.

Balance to close the transaction payable in United States currency by cashier's check drawn on a local bank, subject to prorations or adjustments $50,000.00

Any net differences between the approximate balance of the existing encumbrance shown above and the actual balance at closing to include all unpaid loan payments, accrued interest, late charges, legal fees, taxes, liens, judgments, assessments, and fines shall be adjusted to the purchase price at closing.

All proration computations shall be made as of the previous day before the closing date using the three hundred sixty-five day method. The following items are to be prorated:

1. Real estate taxes for the year of closing. If the taxes for the current year can't be ascertained, any tax proration based on an estimate shall be readjusted on receipt of the tax bill on condition that a statement to that effect is in the closing statement.

2. All statutory liens and assessments recorded against the property as of the closing date shall be paid by the Seller.

3. All water, sewage, electricity, natural gas, and other similar utility charges.

4. Rents due from tenants of the property, as set forth on the rent roll. Seller shall be entitled to receive rent payments for the period up to the day before closing. Buyer shall be entitled

FORM 20.2   Sample Real Estate Purchase Agreement *(Continued)*

to receive all rent payments from and including the day of closing. All rents shall be prorated on the basis of rents actually received.

Seller shall furnish to Buyer copies of all rental agreements and an estoppel letter from each tenant specifying the nature and time of occupancy, amount of rent, and advance rent and security deposits paid.

At the closing, Seller shall deliver the following to the Buyer:

1. Possession of the property, subject to those rental agreements set forth on the rent roll. Delivery of possession of the property shall not be subject to the rights of any other person or entity.

2. Bill of sale for all personal property.

3. Assignment of all tenant rental agreements.

4. All tenant security deposits.

5. A valid certificate of occupancy issued by the appropriate government agency.

6. All blueprints, surveys, and keys to the property.

7. Rent roll listing all tenants residing at the property.

8. All insurance policies and mortgage documents being assumed by the Buyer.

Title to the property shall be conveyed from Seller to Buyer by warranty deed at the closing.

Buyer may assign or otherwise transfer any of Buyer's rights, title, and interest in and to this Purchase Agreement without the Seller's consent.

Buyer and Seller authorize Mr. John B. Good, Attorney at Law, to act as Escrow Agent to receive, deposit, and hold funds and other items in escrow, subject to clearance, disburse them on proper authorization and in accordance with the terms of this Real Estate Purchase Agreement.

IN WITNESS WHEREOF, Seller has set his hand the date aforesaid.

<u>David D. Jones</u>	_____
Seller	Buyer
<u>Robert B. Big</u>	_____
Witness	Witness
<u>Sally M. Little</u>	_____
Witness	Witness

purposes of RESPA are: "To help consumers become better shoppers for settlement services and to eliminate kickbacks and referral fees that unnecessarily increase the costs of certain settlement services." To learn more about RESPA, log on to the following web page: www.hud.gov/offices/hsg/sfh/res/respa_hm.cfm.

Four Things That Must Be Done in Conjunction with the Closing

Once you have scheduled the closing date, the following four things must be done in conjunction with the closing:

1. *Have all utility meters read on the day before closing.* When you are closing on the purchase of a property under option, on the day before the closing, have all the public and private utility companies providing services that the property owner is responsible for paying read their meters. You must notify utility service providers that the property is under new ownership so that you do not get billed for utility services that were provided to the previous owner.

2. *Have the property taxes prorated using the 365-day method.* The only item that cannot be calculated and included on the HUD 1 Settlement Statement at the time it is signed by the optionor and optionee is the amount of the property tax prorations. Property tax prorations cannot be calculated until the actual sale date is known. However, I always stipulate on the settlement statement that the property taxes are to be prorated using the 365-day method. This method of proration is based on the assumption that every year has 365 days. For example, if the annual property tax bill for a small rental property is $4,200 and the seller owned the property for 270 days, the seller's prorated portion of the tax would be $3,108 ($4,200 ÷ 365 days = $11.51 per day × 270 days). However, if the property taxes for the current year cannot be ascertained, stipulate in the closing statement that any tax proration based on an estimate shall be readjusted on receipt of the tax bill.

3. *Close the transaction on the last day of the month.* If you are closing on the purchase of any type of rental property, I recommend that you close the transaction on the last day of the month. This way, you will be in possession of the property on the first day of the month when rental payments generally are due. And you can collect rental payments and initiate eviction proceedings against tenants who do not pay. In addition, closing the sale on the last day of the month eliminates the need to prorate rental payments.

4. *Conduct a final walk-around inspection of the property on the day of the closing.* On the day of the closing, do a final walk-around inspection of the property to double-check for any last-minute changes to the property that could adversely affect its value. I suggest that you do as I do and bring a camera along and look for:
    *   Condemnation notices posted on the property.
    *   Bodies of standing water on the property that cannot drain.
    *   Visible signs that the property is infested with termites or rodents.
    *   Visible signs of environmental hazards on the property.
    *   Code violation notices posted on the property.

Please listen to what I am telling you here about doing a final walk-around inspection on the day of the closing. I will never forget the time that I pulled up in front of a small commercial property one hour before the closing and was met with the pungent smell of raw sewage. Upon further inspection, I found a pool of sewage behind the building. Later on at the closing, I found out from the owner that whenever the municipal sewer line backed up into a section of old Orangeburg sewer pipe on the property, which had been ruptured by root intrusion, the rear of the property became an open sewer. I took a couple of pictures of the mess with my Polaroid camera and headed off to the closing. Needless to say, I was not in the best of humor when I confronted the owner and showed her the pictures. Her response was: "Oh, I thought I told you about that; it only happens when the city sewer backs up." I proceeded to calmly tell her that the deal was off unless I received a $1,500 sewer repair credit on the spot. She quickly agreed to reduce the sale price of the property by $1,500. We went ahead and closed on the sale of the property, and I had the sewer line replaced with six-inch PVC pipe for $1,200. The point that I want to make here is that if I had not taken the time to do a walk-around inspection on the morning of the closing, I would have been out of luck. And my only recourse would have been to take my chances and file a lawsuit against the owner for failure to disclose this health hazard when she completed and signed a property disclosure statement at the same time she signed the option agreement.

Best to Use a Closing Checklist to Catch Potential Problems before the Sale Closes

I always use a buyer's closing checklist, like the one on page 214, to make certain that I do not overlook any of the important details that are an integral part of the closing process. Closing is the time when it is critical that all of your t's are

---

FORM 20.3   Sample Buyer's Closing Checklist

---

1. Review the title insurance policy for exceptions, which are excluded from coverage.

2. Review the survey of the property.

3. Verify the property's legal description.

4. Verify the property's zoning designation.

5. Check with government agencies for building, fire, safety, and health code violations.

6. Review the hazard insurance policy.

7. Review the termite inspection report.

8. Verify the property tax payment status.

9. Compute the mortgage or deed of trust interest proration.

10. Compute the real property tax proration.

11. Check with government agencies for environmental hazard citations.

12. Review the bill of sale for personal property.

13. Review the deed.

14. Review the promissory note.

15. Review the mortgage or deed of trust loan documents.

16. Review the loan assumption documents.

17. Review the HUD 1 Settlement Statement.

18. Verify that a current certificate of occupancy has been issued for the property.

19. Check with government agencies for municipal liens.

---

crossed and your i's dotted. I say this because it can be extremely hard to get mistakes corrected after the closing has taken place, especially when the sellers have picked up stakes and left town without leaving a forwarding address. And when this happens, you are what is known in Marine Corps parlance as SOL!

And while you are doing your pre-closing checks, be sure to take the time to sit down and double-check all loan, title transfer, and closing documents for:

1. Mistakes made in computing prorations.
2. Mistakes made in transposing numbers and letters.
3. Mistakes made in spelling and typing.

Review Your HUD 1 Settlement Statement on the Day before the Closing

Under RESPA, the buyer and seller are allowed to review their HUD 1 Settlement Statement 24 hours in advance of the scheduled closing date. The last time that I used a title insurance company to act as my closing agent, I found a bogus $250 document preparation fee tacked on to my HUD 1, even though the title insurer did not prepare any title transfer documents. The title agent who made the calculations tried to explain the $250 overcharge as an "honest mistake." Sure it was! You can review and fill out a HUD 1 Settlement Statement online at my web site on the following web page: www.thomaslucier.com/HUD1SettlementStatement.pdf.

Though following is a listing of over 100 real estate-related web sites, which every serious option investor should have bookmarked on his or her personal computer.

Property Records Online

Public Record Finder, www.publicrecordfinder.com/property.html
Public Records Sources, www.publicrecordsources.com
Access Central, www.access-central.com
Real Estate Public Records, www.real-estate-public-records.com
Search Systems, www.searchsystems.net
Tax Assessor Database, www.pubweb.acns.nwu.edu/~cap440/assess.html
Public Records Online, www.netronline.com/public_records.htm
National Association of Counties, www.naco.org/counties/counties
Public Records USA, www.factfind.com/public.htm
International Association of Assessing Officers, www.iaao.org/1234.html
Public Records Research System, www.brbpub.com

People Information Online

Internet Address Finder, www.iaf.net
Switchboard, www.switchboard.com
Skipease, www.skipease.com
Social Security Administration Death Index, www.ancestry.com/search/rectype/vital/ssdi/main.htm
Street Address Information, www.melissadate.com/lookups/index.htm
Reverse Telephone Directory, www.reversephonedirectory.com

Crime Information Online

Crime.com, www.crime.com/info/crime_stats/crime_stats.html
Neighborhood crime check, www.apbnews.com/resourcecenter/datacenter/index.html
Nationwide sex registry, www.crimetime.com/bbosex.htm

Environmental Hazardous Waste Information Online

EPA superfund hazardous waste site search, www.epa.gov/superfund/sites/query
/basic.htm
Environmental hazards zip code search, www.scorecard.org
EPA Enviromapper zip code search, www.epa.gov/cgi-bin/enviro/em/empact
/getZipCode.cgi?appl=empact&info=zipcode
HUD environmental maps, www.hud.gov/offices/cio/emaps/index.cfm

Demographic Information Online

FFIEC Geocoding System, www.ffiec.gov/geocode/default.htm
U.S. Census Bureau FactFinder, www.factfinder.census.gov/servlet/BasicFactsServlet
U.S. Census Bureau Gazetteer, www.census.gov/cgi-bin/gazetteer
U.S. Census Bureau QuickFacts, www.quickfacts.census.gov/qfd/index.html
U.S. Census Bureau zip code statistics, www.census.gov/epcd/www/zipstats.html

Maps Online

MapQuest, www.mapquest.com
MapBlast, www.mapblast.com
Maptech, www.mapserver.maptech.com
Expedia, www.expedia.com
Topozone, adwww.tpozone.com
Yahoo Maps, adwww.maps.yahoo.com
Maps, www.maps.com

Title Insurance Information Online

American Land Title Association, www.alta.org
TitleWeb, www.titleweb.com
Old Republic National Title Insurance Company, www.orlink.oldrepnatl.com/index.htm
Stewart Title Insurance Company, www.stewart.com
Chicago Title Insurance Company, www.ctic.com
Fidelity National Title Insurance Company, www.fntic.com
First American Title Insurance Company, www.firstam.com/fatic/html/about
/site-map.html
Lawyers Title Insurance Corporation, www.landam.com/subsidiaries/LTIC/index.asp

Title Insurance Underwriting Information Online

Old Republic National Title Insurance Company, http://orlink.oldrepnatl.com
/Underwriters/pages/Table%20of%20Contents.htm
Chicago Title Insurance Company, www.ctic.com/operations.htm

First American Title Insurance Company, www.firstam.com/faf/reference /uwtools.html
Stewart Title Virtual Underwriter, www.vuwriter.com

Attorney Locator Services Online

Martindale Hubbell Lawyer Locator, www.martindale.com/locator/home.html
Findlaw, www.findlaw.com/14firms
Lawyers, www.lawyers.com

Comparable Residential Property Sales Data Online

DataQuick, www.dataquick.com
HomeGain, www.homegain.com
REAL-COMP, www.real-comp.com
HomeRadar, www.homeradar.com
Domania Home Price Check, www.domania.com

Comparable Commercial Property Sale and Income Data Online

CoStar Exchange, www.costar.com
Loopnet, www.loopnet.com
National Real Estate Index, www,realestateindex.com
IDM Corporation, www.idmdata-now.com
DataQuick, www.dataquick.com
Apartment Comparable Sales, www.apartmentcomps.com
Real Estate Information Source, www.reis.com

Renters' Insurance Information Online

InsWeb, www.insweb.comQuoteFetcher
Quote Fetcher, www.quotefetcher.com/renters-insurance.htm
NETQUOTE, www.netquote.com
Geico Renters' Insurance, www.homeowners.geico.com/renters.html

Property Replacement Cost Information Online

Marshall & Swift, www.marshallswift.com
Craftsman Book Company, www.craftsman-book.com
R.S. Means Company, www.rsmeans.com

Construction Cost Calculator, www.get-a-quote.net
Construction Material Calculators, www.constructionworkcenter.com
/calculators.html
Building Cost Calculator, www.nt.receptive.com/rsmeans/calculator

Property Appraisal Information Online

Appraisal Foundation, www.appraisalfoundation.org
Appraisal Institute, www.appraisalinstitute.org
Federal Appraisal Subcommittee, www.asc.gov
Real Estate Appraisal Books, www.rwm.net/books.htm
Appraisers Forum, www.appraisersforum.com
Appraisal Today, www.appraisaltoday.com
American Society of Appraisers, www.appraisers.org
National Association of Independent Fee Appraisers, www.naifa.com

Property Valuation and
Analysis Software Online

Z-Law Real Estate Software Catalog, www.z-law.com
Real Estate Valuation Software, www.atvalue.com
Real Data Real Estate Software, www.realdata.com

Tax Information Online

Internal Revenue Service, www.irs.gov
Internal Revenue Service Forms and Publications, www.irs.gov/formspubs/index.html
Internal Revenue Code and Tax Regulations Online, www.tax.cchgroup.com
/freecoderegs
Revenue Ruling Bulletins, www.irs.gov/businfo/bullet.html
Technical Advice Memorandums, www.apps.irs.gov/news/efoia/determine.html

Credit Reporting Agencies Online

Equifax Credit Information Services, www.equifax.com
Trans Union, LLC, www.transunion.com
Experian Consumer Credit Services, www.experian.com
Dunn & Bradstreet Business Information Reports, www.dnb.com
Experian Business Profile Reports, www.experian.com

Lead-Based Paint Hazard Information Online

EPA National Lead Information Center, www.epa.gov/lead/nlic.htm
Lead-Based Paint Disclosure Fact Sheet, www.epa.gov/opptintr/lead/fs-discl.pdf
Lessor's Lead-Based Paint Disclosure Statement, www.epa.gov/opptintr/lead/lesr_eng.pdf

HUD Lead-Based Paint Abatement Guidelines, www.lead-info.com
/abatementguidelinesexamp.html
EPA Lead information Pamphlet, www.hud.gov/lea/leapame.pdf

Indoor Mold Information Online

EPA Mold Resources, www.epa.gov/iaq/pubs/moldresources.html
EPA Sick Building Syndrome, www.epa.gov/iaq/pubs/sbs.html
Mold and Fungi Assessment and Remediation, www.nyc.gov/html/doh/html
/epi/moldrpt1.html

Building and Repair Cost Calculators Online

Construction Material Calculators, www.constructionworkcenter.com/calculators.html
Building Cost Calculator, www.nt.receptive.com/rsmeans/calculator
Construction Cost Calculator, www.get-a-quote.net

Commercial Property Sales Online

Real Buyer, www.realbuyer.net
Biz Trader, www.biztrader.com
REBUZ, www.rebuz.com
Loopnet, www.loopnet.com
Post Your Property, www.postyourproperty.com
Apartments for Sale, www.apartmentsales.com
Land Net, www.land.net
Realty Investor, www.realtyinvestor.com
Dealmakers Commercial Property Forum, commercial-realestate@dealmakers.net
Dealmakers Investment Property Forum, Investment-realestate@dealmakers.net

Real Estate-Related Information Online

American Society of Home Inspectors, www.ashi.org/find
First American Real Estate Solutions, www.firstamres.com/html/home.asp
Abstracters Online, www.abstractersonline.com
Comprehensive Loss Underwriting Exchange, www.choicepoint.net
Waste Management, www.wm.com
Dumpsters USA, www.dumpstersusa.com
Commerce Clearinghouse, http://tax.cchgroup.com
HUD 1 Settlement Statement, www.thomaslucier.com/HUD1SettlementStatement.pdf
Nightingale-Conant, www.nightingale.com
North American Loan Servicing, www.sellerloans.com/index.htm
PLM Lender Services, Inc., www.plmweb.com/index.html
Planning Commission Information, www. plannersweb.com
Real Estate Glossary, www.realestatejournal.com/partners/reglossary

Thomas J. Lucier has been a real estate investor in Tampa, Florida, since 1980. Mr. Lucier is the author of six books on real estate investing and managing Florida residential rental property. He is also a Florida licensed mortgage broker, and an active member of the National Association of Real Estate Editors and the Real Estate Educators Association. Mr. Lucier's real estate investment advice has been published in the *Wall Street Journal, Commercial Investment Real Estate* magazine, and on CBS MarketWatch and Bankrate web sites. To read more about Thomas J. Lucier, log on to his web site at www.thomaslucier.com.

Unlike 99 percent of all real estate authors in America, there are no gatekeepers between Thomas J. Lucier and his readers. Tom answers his own e-mail and telephone, and is fully wired to communicate from anywhere within the United States. You can e-mail Thomas J. Lucier directly at tjlucier@thomaslucier.com, or you can call Tom at his office in Tampa, Florida, at (813) 237-6267, to speak with him personally.